SO YOU THINK YOU KNOW MAINE

Books by Neil Rolde

York Is Living History

Sir William Pepperrell of Colonial New England

Rio Grande do Norte: The Story of Maine's Partner State in Brazil

So You Think You Know Maine

SO
You Think
YOU
Know Maine

Neil Rolde / York   WCBB / Lewiston

Harpswell Press

Gardiner

Library of Congress Catalog Card Number 84-47758

ISBN: 0-88448-025-9

Third Printing

Designed on Crummett Mountain by Edith Allard

Index prepared by John N. Ferdico

Harpswell Press
Gardiner, Maine 04345

Manufactured in the United States of America

ACKNOWLEDGMENTS

Charles Jacobs of Dexter, Maine, my successor as staff assistant in Governor Kenneth M. Curtis's office and later an assistant to U.S. Senators Edmund S. Muskie and George Mitchell, first broached the idea to me of doing a book of "So You Think You Know Maine." To "Charley" Jacobs, then, I am indebted for the initial impulse that led to this venture, although it took a number of years to germinate into full-fledged reality.

Gathering the material for a project this complicated required the help of many persons, particularly in assembling the necessary pictures. I would like to thank especially:

Henry Harding of York, Maine
Susan Rayfield of the Maine Arts and Humanities Commission
Earle Shettleworth, Frank Beard and Bob Bradley of the Maine Historic Preservation Commission
Paul Rivard of the Maine State Museum
Bob Deis of the Maine Department of Agriculture
Dick Dyer of the Maine Department of Conservation
Tom Shoener of the Maine Fisheries and Wildlife Department
The Maine Marine Resources Department
The Maine Publicity Bureau
Rep. Susan Bell of South Paris
Ed Pert, Clerk of the Maine House of Representatives
Harriet Passerman and Odell Skinner of WCBB
Randy Tunks of Central Photo Lab, State of Maine
L.L. Bean Company

Contents

BY WAY OF BACKGROUND

Armistice Day, November 11, 1975, was more important in Maine than just an occasion for celebrating the 57th anniversary of the end of World War I. At 8:30 that evening, a new television program was launched in the state, something different, produced locally. The show was entitled "So You Think You Know Maine" and it had been fashioned by Channel 10, Maine's pioneer public television station, a joint venture of the state's three most prestigious private colleges, Colby, Bates and Bowdoin (which accounts for its call letters, WCBB).

Designed as a quiz program to test Maine people's knowledge of their own state, "So You Think You Know Maine" was introduced in part as a contribution to the nation's Bicentennial Celebration, then underway. An avowed purpose, according to the first publicity blurbs, was to find "Maine's Master of Memorabilia" — in other words, a contestant hardy enough to survive the weekly and monthly rounds of searching questions on every aspect of Maine life.

From the start, "So You Think You Know Maine" was a hit. The initial show had somewhat of a different format than it has now — proof that like all good things even a TV quiz program can evolve toward greater perfection

Originally, the show had two distinct sections, Part I and Part II. A panel of four contestants in the first Part were asked "Toss-Up Questions" — random queries that had to be answered competitively. Whoever buzzed ahead of the others and was correct received five points and went on to the Hodge-Podge Board where the questions were in categories and worth ten points. In Part II, called the "Lights of Fortune Round," the top two survivors of Part I were tested with further category questions, covering subjects that ranged from Maine government to Down East slang.

Andy Jensen, a young former radio announcer, was the first host. After two years, he gave way to Jeff Gabel who ever since has been the show's master of ceremonies. Gabel, a native Pennsylvanian, came to Maine after a varied career that included a stint as a professional clown with the Florida-based Hoxie Brothers Circus. Now settled in Sabattus and able to cope with the Maine pronounciations that threw him off at first, the affable Gabel, who is also a singer and actor, has proven to be one of the most popular features of "So You Think You Know Maine."

The idea for the program came from Odell Skinner, then, as now, WCBB's station manager. Harry Wiest was the producer-director and Laurie Manny the program coordinator who pulled everything together for this ground-breaking broadcasting effort. Help in research and on the accuracy of questions came from the Maine League of Historical Societies and Museums.

The very first four contestants were Hope Ryan of Hampden, Bradbury Blake of South Paris, George Shur of Portland and Philip Wilder of Brunswick. Bradbury Blake was the first weekly winner.

The very first "Master of Memorabilia" was Bruce Livingston of Augusta.

Eight years later, "So You Think You Know Maine" has an audience of more than 35,000 in the Pine Tree State. It has been modified to include three rounds and a number of other new wrinkles, particularly in the area of visual questions. The most significant addition is the children's version, which presently runs as frequently as the adult show. No less an outfit than the Corporation for Public Broadcasting has honored WCBB for its children's version of "So You Think You Know Maine" — not once but twice, both in 1981 and 1983!

Over the years, "So You Think You Know Maine" has developed a loyal and often even fanatical following — fanatical in the sense that they are quick to pounce upon the slightest error of fact in the questioning and have no hesitation about letting the station know if it has goofed.

Thus, the flurry of letters from citizens of Moscow, Maine when it was rashly stated over the air that the location of the

Central Maine Power Company's massive Wyman Dam was in the town of Bingham. The First Selectman of Moscow fired off a letter tartly stating that "the last time we looked, the dam was still located here in Moscow." However, some of his constituents were even more accurate, pin-pointing the fact that Wyman Dam runs between Moscow and Pleasant Ridge Plantation, with its main entrance in Moscow.

Another brouhaha developed over the name of the highest peak in the Camden Hills State Park. A contestant answered Mount Megunticook, but he was ruled incorrect. The host declared that it was Mount Battie. A flood of letters followed, showing that Mount Megunticook on the park's own trail map was listed as 1,380 feet high while Mount Battie was a mere 900 feet, so that the contestant's original answer had not been wrong.

The tone of these and other corrections, it must be added, is usually good-natured and rarely irate. Rather, it seems to follow in the Maine tradition of wanting to help out a neighbor by gently but firmly establishing a course of right guidance. Nor are errors frequent. The program goes to considerable pains to assure the accuracy of its answers. Also, the depth of viewer interest is so intense that many questions are derived from viewer contributions; indeed, a whole category of "Viewer Questions" was early developed.

Various celebrities — Maine celebrities, that is — have appeared on the show. One of the finalists in the beginning years was Earle G. Shettleworth, Jr., now the director of the Maine Historic Preservation Commission. The Maine State Historian, Dr. Robert York, has been a contestant several times. One memorable show pitted writer Bill Caldwell, sportsmen's columnist Bud Leavitt, TV personality Lew Colby, and Dick Anderson, the present Commissioner of the Maine Department of Conservation. Anderson won. Portland Mayor Linda Abromson has been on the show as has Portland restaurateur Parker Reidy. Humorists Joe Perham and Newt Hinckley have participated. A spirited rivalry occurred one time between Ed Gorham, secretary-treasurer of the Maine AFL-CIO and State Representative Dick Davies of Orono, who is currently an assistant to Governor Joseph E. Brennan.

Now, "So You Think You Know Maine" is entering a new media — print — and this popular weekly television game, through this publication, can be played at home, and with its WHAT YOU OUGHT TO KNOW ABOUT MAINE sections and other information provided, can serve as a source book and educational reference as well as a vehicle for entertainment.

The motto of the State of Maine is a Latin phrase that means "I lead." What is that motto?

If you answered "Dirigo," you are correct.

And the motto stands as an apt one for the state, seeing that in many areas throughout its past Maine has led the nation in governmental innovations, economic developments and here, in truth, in public television programming.

"So You Think You Know Maine" was a first of its kind for the country. Its continued success demonstrates that it has touched a popular nerve among Maine people, proud of their state and eager to have ever more knowledge of our unique corner of the United States.

HOW TO PLAY

Start with Round I. One player should be chosen as host to control the questions and answers. Correct answers are printed on the reverse side of each page of questions.

As much as possible, the game follows the format of the TV show. A Toss-Up Question is selected by the host. Whoever is the first to answer it correctly receives five points. Subtract five points for an incorrect answer. The person who has answered the Toss-Up Question correctly then has a chance to pick a Category Question in Round I. Score ten points for a correct answer to a Category Question, but no loss of points for an incorrect answer. If no one answers the first Toss-Up Question correctly, go on to a second Toss-Up Question. Again, if the Toss-Up has been answered correctly, the person who does this can choose a Category Question to answer.

Every Round of play must include six Toss-Up Questions and a potential of six Category Questions. In addition, each Round must have one Pens-in-Hand Question, one Visual Question and one Essay Question, which are asked of all the players. Score five points for a correct Pens-in-Hand answer and five points for a correct Visual Question answer, with no penalty for guessing wrong. The Essay Question is broken down into five sub-questions, each worth two points. Here, however, subtract two points for every mistake. If you can't answer correctly on something you've just read or had read to you, you deserve to lose points.

After you finish Round I, go on to Round II and then to Round III.

The player with the highest cumulative score at the end of Round III wins.

The answers impart a good deal of information. The host may wish to read some or all of this information to the players. An object of the game, aside from winning and having fun, is also to learn some new things about Maine and stimulate one's curiosity about our state.

There are no penalties for stopping along the way to read the WHAT YOU OUGHT TO KNOW ABOUT MAINE sections, or to look at any of the pictures.

When the questions in the book — and there are a lot of them — are exhausted, material is furnished so that players can make up their own questions.

If you play without a host or by yourself, we can't do much about it if you cheat and peek at the answers ahead of time. But we know you won't!

Also, if you want to play the game any other way than what we suggest, it won't hurt our feelings. We urge you to be as creative as you like.

A QUICKY

In a small Maine town, Old Bert had the reputation of being a terrible liar. One day, a bunch of fellows were sitting around in Charley Fernald's store when Old Bert came by. Charley yelled to him jokingly, "Hey, Bert, come on in and tell us a lie."

"I can't," Old Bert shouted back to Charley. "Your father just fell and broke his leg at home and I'm on my way to get the doctor for him."

Upset, Charley rushed off to find his aged father perfectly fit — and, within about half a minute, himself pretty angry over Old Bert's "Dod-blowed lie."

This is a true Maine story from Down East. Only the names have been fictionalized.

ROUND

Toss-Up Questions

1 In 19th century Maine, this day was considered the social event of the year. Families became reacquainted with distant neighbors, and while the men took care of the town's business and politics, the women set out a festive noon day meal. What annual event was attended with great enthusiasm? It is still important in Maine today and usually falls within the month of March.

2 What organization am I? I was formed all over Maine in the 1870's to promote better farming methods. On the county level, I am called a "Pomona." I was influential in establishing R.F.D. mail delivery in Maine.

3 Three Indian tribes were involved in Maine's famous Indian land claims case that was settled in 1980. The Penobscots and the Passamaquoddies are the best known of these tribes. What is the third tribe?

4 In 1779, during the American Revolution, an entire American fleet was lost in the course of attempting to re-capture Castine from the British. Name the expedition.

5 Governor James B. Longley, Maine's only independent governor, did something more often than any other previous governor. In fact, he did it 109 times. What did he do?

6 In what year did forest fires burn thousands of acres in Maine (particularly in York County) and nearly destroy several communities, including Bar Harbor?

Answers to Toss-Up Questions

1 Annual Town Meeting Day.

The venerable institution of the town meeting in Maine was actually an importation from Massachusetts. The original forms of government proposed for Maine were far more aristocratic, being based on the right of the grantee of land from the king to govern pretty much as he chose. Sir Ferdinando Gorges, in his "Palatinate of Maine" had virtually the powers of a monarch.

2 The Grange.

Officially known as the National Grange of the Patrons of Husbandry, this nationwide movement began in the farmlands of the Middle West in 1867. It gradually moved east and during the 1870's acquired considerable political clout, capturing several state legislatures and passing laws to benefit farmers. It came to Maine in 1873.

3 The Malecites (pronounced MALASEATS).

The Malacites of Maine, members of a larger Canadian-based tribe, are centered in the Houlton area of Aroostook County. They do not have a specific reservation, unlike the Penobscots and Passamaquoddies who have been recognized by treaties with the State of Maine and even have official representatives (non-voting) to the Maine Legislature.

4 The Penobscot Expedition.

An expedition of 19 armed ships and 24 transports under Commodore Dudley Saltonstall met a disastrous defeat in the Penobscot River. Saltonstall was courtmartialed for his role in this fiasco. Exonerated was Paul Revere, who took part as a colonel in charge of ordnance. Recently, the Maine State Museum has undertaken a program of underwater archaeology at the site of the battle.

5 Vetoed legislation.

Out of 109 vetoes by Governor Longley, 56 were overridden by the Legislature. One was even overridden unanimously by the House, prompting one veteran lawmaker to quip that "This was our first shutout."

6 1947.

Wildfire Loose: The Week That Maine Burned is the title of a recent book describing the summer and early fall of that year when near drought conditions led to disastrous fires. As a result of these events, Maine government initiated a statewide program of forest fire supression that continues to this day.

Toss-Up Questions

7 Here is an old remedy that was used by sailors in Maine. What was it supposed to cure?

A good sized piece of pork is tied to the end of a long string. While one sailor holds onto the string, the suffering crew member swallows the piece of pork. Then, at the proper moment, the piece of pork is yanked out.

8 The names of three Maine counties honor heroes of the American Revolution. Identify them.

9 Another county question. What Maine county can be identified by the following clues?

"I am Maine's second largest county."

"I contain the highest mountain in Maine."

"I am the most sparsely populated county in the state."

"My name, when translated from the Algonquian Indian language into English, means *rapid waters*."

10 Ferdinand W. Demara, Jr. led an interesting life. In fact, he inspired a film that starred Tony Curtis in the title role. Demara's last exploit took place on North Haven Island in Maine. What was Demara's claim to fame?

11 The first settlement in Maine was on St. Croix Island. By what other name is this island known?

12 Chester Greenwood of Farmington is noted for having invented ear muffs. What automotive invention is also credited to him.?

7 Seasickness.

Resorting to such a rather extreme bit of business was also supposed to cure nausea or dizziness. At first blush, it appears to an objective observer that it might have had the opposite effect, at least where *nausea* is concerned.

8 Knox, Hancock, Washington.

Of the three, Henry Knox, America's first secretary of war, had the closest ties to Maine. He married the granddaughter of Samuel Waldo and inherited through her large properties in mid-coast Maine. A replica of his stately home, "Montpelier," can still be seen today at Thomaston. John Hancock, first governor of Massachusetts after the Revolution, was, of course, also simultaneously governor of Maine. Before the Revolution, he had important business ties here. The Hancock warehouse, where allegedly he hid smuggled goods from the British, is now a museum at York. George Washington, while commanding colonial troops in Boston, conferred with the Maine Indian chief Joseph Orono and won his allegiance to the American cause.

9 Piscataquis County.

Piscataquis County contains 3,809.5 square miles, 85 percent of which is forested. The highest mountain is Katahdin, 5,267 feet. The county's population in 1980 was 17,612, which is 1.6 percent of the state's total. Placed within 12.5 percent of the state's land area, this gives Piscataquis County a population density of five persons per square mile, the lowest in Maine.

10 He was the "Great Imposter."

Without any training or proper credentials, Demara successfully posed and practiced as a priest, a doctor, a prison official, a military officer and a teacher until he was exposed. In Maine, he served as a teacher in a remote rural school.

11 Dochet Island.

In 1604, the French aristocrat, Pierre du Guast, landed a party of colonists on this island in the St. Croix River. The group of 70 men, which included several priests, passed the winter there and celebrated the first Christmas in the New World. Deciding that the site was a poor one, they soon moved on to a better location in Canada.

12 Shock absorbers.

Greenwood was recently honored by the Maine Legislature, who set aside the one hundredth anniversary of his birth as "Chester Greenwood Day" throughout the state, an act that received nationwide attention.

13 Maine ranks second in the nation in its high percentage of French-speaking people. What state ranks first?

14 There are a number of Maine municipalities that share names with cities and towns in England, Italy and Greece, and even with those of entire foreign countries. But there is only one Maine community that has the same name as a city in Spain. Name it.

15 They wear blue uniforms while they're working.
  In the fall, they wear bright red jackets and fluorescent orange vests.
  They're found on both water and land. They enforce laws. Who are they?

16 According to the Maine Constitution, what elected official succeeds a governor who dies in office?

17 What do the following clues describe?
  They can legally be taken from coastal waters between November 1 and April 15.
  Knights returning from the Crusades wore them as a badge of honor.
  They have curved, deeply grooved shells.
  They are very tasty.
  They are identified with St. James.

18 The two men responsible for the signing of the treaty that settled the Aroostook War were Daniel Webster and Alexander Baring. True or False?

Answers to Toss-Up Questions

13 Louisiana.

It is estimated that 14.2 percent of Maine's population consider French their mother tongue. Van Buren, in the St. John Valley of Aroostook County, has the highest percentage of French speakers — 93.9 percent. The French-speaking population of Louisiana is descended largely from Acadians who were forced out of Nova Scotia by the British in the 1750's. Maine's French-speaking population is made up of Acadians in the north and the descendants of those who came from Quebec province to the cities in the 19th century.

14 Madrid. (pronounced MAD-rid, not MA-drid)

The famous road sign in Albany with many foreign names on it is one of the most photographed tourist attractions in Maine. To the places like Naples, Canton, Denmark, Sweden, Peru, Paris, etc. on this sign, one can add communities elsewhere in the state like Athens, Corinth, Rome, Stockholm, Lisbon, etc. Some of these foreign names are pronounced in a peculiar Maine fashion, as MAD-RID is. Thus, Mainers don't call Calais CALLAY like the French do, but CALLUS. There are some other Spanish names in Maine besides Madrid, but you'd hardly know it. Casco Bay, for example, comes from *Bahia de Casco*, meaning a helmet-shaped bay, and the Bay of Fundy from *Bahia Profundo*, meaning deep bay. These names were bestowed on them by an early Spanish explorer of the Maine coast, Esteban Gomez.

15 Maine's game wardens.

The laws they enforce as part of the Department of Inland Fisheries and Wildlife are those passed by the Legislature or promulgated as rules by the Department for the protection of Maine's animal resources. There are 90 game wardens in the field, seventeen sergeants, five lieutenants and 23 deputy game wardens.

16 The president of the State Senate.

17 Sea scallops.

In 1979, Maine fishermen landed 1,163,645 pounds of sea scallop meats with a value of $3,878,413.

18 True.

Daniel Webster, the U.S. secretary of state, and Alexander Baring, Lord Ashburton, a British banker, negotiated the Webster-Ashburton Treaty of 1842 thereby settling a potentially explosive boundary dispute in northern Maine. Baring was married to an American, the daughter of Robert Bingham of Philadelphia, who owned vast tracts of land in Maine. The town of Baring in Washington County is named for him. Although the United States received 7,000 square miles of the disputed territory, the people of Maine were not happy with the treaty, feeling they should have gotten more.

Toss-Up Questions

19 James G. Blaine, one of Maine's most famous politicians, was the Republican nominee for President of the United States in 1884. He narrowly lost that election to what rather rotund Democrat?

20 The S.P.A. is the governing body for high school athletics in the State of Maine. What do the initials S.P.A. stand for?

21 To what were the Puritans of 1750 referring when they passed the following law?

"They have a pernicious influence on the minds of young people and greatly endanger their morals by giving them a taste for intrigue, amusement and pleasure. Therefore, their doors shall be closed!"

22 What animal am I?

"I eat enormous amounts of spiders, insects and berries."

"I am a small gray and white bird with a black patch on the top of my head."

"In 1927, I was named the State bird of Maine."

23 Queen Victoria of England knighted Hiram Maxim in 1901. For what reason was this American-born inventor, originally from Sangerville, Maine, so honored?

24 Where would you be most likely to encounter "grunters" and "groaners?"

Along the sea coast?

On a lily pad?

At an FM radio station?

19 Grover Cleveland.

James Gillespie Blaine. 1830–93, was born in Pennsylvania, but moved to Maine as a young man. He taught school prior to becoming editor of the Kennebec Journal. A founder of Maine's Republican Party, he soon became prominent in politics. As a congressman and U.S. senator, he rose within his party's ranks. Charges of corruption against Blaine contained in the so-called "Mulligan Letters" cost him the Republican nomination for president in 1876. As the G.O.P.'s nominee in 1884, he might have won against Cleveland had it not been for the tactless remark of a supporter in New York who called the Democrats the party of "Rum, Romanism and Rebellion." This alienated the Irish Catholic vote in New York; Blaine lost the Empire State by 1,000 votes, and with it, the election. His former home in Augusta, the Blaine House, now serves as the residence for Maine's governors.

20 The State Principals' Association.*

Since 1934–35, the S.P.A. has handled all of the statewide and regional tournaments for high school athletics. In recent years, it has merged with the State Coaches Association in performing these activities. The basketball tournaments, now for girls as well as boys, are the most popular of the events, but the S.P.A. handles some 16 different sports. It also has responsibility for 6 non-athletic school activities, including the overseeing of debate contests, the honor society, etc.

21 Theaters or playhouses.

The "Drama Law of 1750," outlawed theatrical performances in Massachusetts and Maine. Early Puritan prejudices also extended to the celebration of Christmas, which was considered blasphemous. Before its absorption by Massachusetts, Maine served as a refuge for those fleeing the rigorous social rules of the Puritan Commonwealth to the south. One of the most noted refugees was Thomas Morton of Quincy, who, according to Nathaniel Hawthorne, was persecuted because he allowed dancing around a maypole. There is evidence, however, that Morton sold rum and guns to the Indians.

22 The black-capped chickadee.

23 Maxim invented the modern machine gun.

Hiram Stevens Maxim was born at Sangerville, Maine in 1840. In addition to inventing the Maxim machine gun, he developed a smokeless powder, a delayed action fuse and a heavier-than-air airplane. His brother, Hudson Maxim, and his son, Hiram P. Maxim, were also inventors. The latter perfected the silencer for weapons and engines. Also born in the little town of Sangerville was another American destined to be knighted by the British crown — Sir Harry Oakes.

24 Along the sea coast.

A "groaner" is a foghorn with one prolonged tone and a "grunter" is a two-toned foghorn.

*The official title is the Maine State Secondary Schools Principals Association, but is popularly referred to as the S.P.A.

Toss-Up Questions

25 This Oxford County Village is perched 831 feet above sea level and offers a spectacular view of Mount Washington on a clear day. The former home of a onetime Vice President of the United States is located here. Can you name the village?

26 Prior to embarking on a highly successful career as a historical novelist, this Kennebunk native was a columnist for "The Saturday Evening Post" and a noted travel writer. Identify him.

27 Of the more than 400 municipalities in Maine, only a certain number are officially designated as cities. How many cities are there in Maine?

28 Coffee breaks are an important part of the typical Maine work day. What kind of breaks did the Maine working man enjoy during the first half of the 19th century?

29 Until recently, there was something unique about the stop light on Maine Street in Farmington. What was so unusual about it?

30 At the end of the war in 1690–91, which was known in England as King William's War and in New England as Governor Phips' War, only four settlements were left standing in Maine: Wells, York, Kittery and Appledore. Where was Appledore located?

25 Paris Hill.

Part of the town of Paris, Paris Hill village remains much as it did many years ago. It contains the handsome house that belonged to Hannibal Hamlin, who was vice president during Lincoln's first term, 1860–64. Hamlin, a Democrat who converted to a Republican because of his anti-slavery views, was later replaced on the G.O.P. ticket by the southerner Andrew Johnson. Also at Paris Hill is a bell tower in the Baptist Church with a bell in it cast by the Revere Foundry and an Old Stone Jail, now a museum.

26 Kenneth Roberts.

Roberts, born in Kennebunk, was first a newspaperman before turning to other types of writing. His most famous novels include *Northwest Passage*, *Arundel*, *Rabble In Arms*, *Boon Island*, and *Oliver Wiswell*. He won a special Pulitzer Prize citation for his historical novels in 1957.

27 22.

Maine's cities range in size from Portland, with 61,530 people to Eastport, with 1,999 (1980 population). The 22 cities are: Auburn, Augusta, Bangor, Bath, Belfast, Biddeford, Brewer, Calais, Caribou, Eastport, Ellsworth, Gardiner, Hallowell, Lewiston, Old Town, Portland, Presque Isle, Rockland, Saco, South Portland, Waterville, Westbrook.

28 Rum breaks.

There were two of them a day, at 11:00 and 4:00. It's perhaps not surprising that the first prohibition law in the country was passed in Maine. More recently, Maine was the first state in the nation to pass an Alcohol Premium Law, using a special impost on alcoholic beverages in a dedicated fund to combat alcoholism.

29 It was the only stop light in Franklin County.

One of Maine's less populous counties, Franklin, had 27,003 people in 1979. Farmington is the county seat. The town of Strong in Franklin County advertises itself as the toothpick capital of the world and also was the birthplace of the Republican Party in Maine.

30 On the Isles of Shoals.

Eight small islands comprise the Isles of Shoals, whose jurisdiction is split between Maine and New Hampshire. Until the Revolution, a number of these islands, including Appledore, were well populated, but their exposure to British occupation caused them to be evacuated. No one now lives on Appledore year round, although Cornell University maintains a seasonal marine biology station there. Appledore is part of the town of Kittery today.

Toss-Up Questions

31 An Indian chief in Maine was elected by his tribe to serve for which of the following periods of time:

For life?

For a specific number of years depending upon his age?

For only as long as he was doing a good job?

32 Mount Desert is the name of one of Maine's most famous islands. Who was responsible for giving it this unusual name?

33 Picture yourself sitting on Santa Claus's lap in the 19th century. You have established the fact that you have been very good all year and you tell Santa that you want a "coaster" for Christmas. Have you requested a ship, or a 12-man toboggan, or a single, wide ski that looks a little like a modern surfboard and provides a thrilling ride down hard-packed, snow-covered hills?

34 Margaret Chase Smith is one of Maine's most distinguished citizens. While she was serving in the U.S. House and Senate, she always wore a flower pinned to her dress. What type of flower was this and what color was it?

35 In the great seal of the State of Maine, a star surmounts the rest of the design. What does the star represent?

36 What did Artemus Ward and Charles Farrar Browne have in common?

31 For only as long as he was doing a good job.

Today's chiefs of Maine's tribes are called governors and are elected, along with tribal councils. The tradition of keeping a good man in office still continues. John Stevens, governor of the Passamaquoddy reservation at Peter Dana Point in Washington County was first elected when he was seventeen years old and has stayed in office for many, many years. He was also the first Indian to serve as Maine's Commissioner of Indian Affairs. A split among the Penobscot tribe once led to an agreement to alternate governors from the different factions every year.

32 Samuel de Champlain.

After it was decided in 1604 that the French colony on St. Croix Island should be moved, Champlain, as their navigator, was sent out to look for better locations. On this expedition, he explored the Maine coast and in the process named several famous landmarks like Petit Manan and the Isle au Haut. Mount Desert, or in French, "l'Isle des Monts Deserts" ("the island of the desert-like mountains") was so named because of its barren and desolate appearance.

33 A ship.

"Coasters" were sailing vessels confined to the coastal trade along the Maine seaboard. How Santa would manage to get one of them under the tree is another question.

34 A rose and it was always red.

Mrs. Smith, who was first elected to fill out the term of her congressman husband, Clyde Smith, who died in office, was also noted for almost never having missed a roll call. She was the first woman whose name was ever put in nomination for the President of the United States by a major party (at the Republican national Convention of 1964).

35 The North Star.

It denotes the fact that when Maine became a state (1820), it was the northern-most in the Union.

36 They were one and the same person.

As a reporter on the *Cleveland Plain Dealer* in 1858, Browne, who was born in Waterford, Maine began a series of "Artemus Ward's letters" whose humor soon made him famous. He was said to be Abraham Lincoln's favorite humorist. His home in Waterford still stands in the center of town. The pseudonym he used may have been derived from Arte*mas* Ward, a distinguished American Revolutionary War general.

37 Maine's oldest covered bridge was built in 1840. It is located in Cumberland County between Gorham and Windham and it spans the Presumpscot River. Can you name this bridge?

38 A "peavey" is the name of a tool that was invented by a Maine blacksmith, Joseph Peavey, in 1858. In what industry is a "peavey" used?

39 Where would you most likely find a "carapace?"
In a hospital? On a lobster? In a museum?

40 Identify the following town:
"I'm located in Hancock County."
"I was originally settled as a trading post by the Pilgrims of Plymouth."
"I've had French, British, Dutch and American flags fly over me."
"I was named for a French aristocrat who married an Indian girl."

41 Identify the following county:
"I have 889.9 square miles." "I am centrally located in Maine."
"I am divided by the Kennebec River."

42 What Rockland-born, Pulitzer Prize-winning poet wrote these lines?
"My candle burns at both ends:
It will not last the night:
But, ah, my foes, and oh, my friends...
It gives a lovely light!"

37 Babb's Bridge.

In 1973, after a fire at this venerable bridge, the Maine Department of Transportation proposed replacing it with a concrete structure. Legislative pressure forced them to change their plans and the wooden structure was reconstructed.

38 The lumber or logging industry.

The use of the "peavey" was most intense during the log drives on Maine's rivers and lakes. It is a type of pole with an iron contraption at its tip, used for hooking logs and trying to keep them from jamming. In 1971, driving logs on Maine's waterways was prohibited by the Legislature.

39 On a lobster.

The "carapace" is the main body of the lobster, extending from the head of the crustacean to the commencement of its tail and curling around to its underside.

40 Castine.

Jean Vincent de l'Abadie, Baron de St. Castin, a scapegrace offspring of a noble family from the Basque country of France eventually was to give his name to this settlement along Penobscot Bay. The very first white men there were the Pilgrims from Plymouth who went to trade for furs. The French chased them away. At one point, the Dutch conquered the town from the French, only to lose it soon afterward. The British captured it twice — during the Revolution and the War of 1812. Castin was married to the daughter of Madockawando, a famous chief.

41 Kennebec County.

The political heart of Maine lies in Augusta, but this central position was not gained without a long fight with Portland. As late as 1907, Portlanders in the Legislature were still trying to move the capital to their city. Since then, an amendment has been added to the State Constitution, confirming Augusta as the capital. Kennebec County has more than 100 lakes and ponds. It contains almost 10 percent of the state's population.

42 Edna St. Vincent Millay.

In 1923, Edna St. Vincent Millay won the Pulitzer Prize for her volume of poetry entitled *The Ballad of the Harp Weaver*. Noted for the lyric quality of her sonnets, she was one of the most popular poets of her day. She was a playwright, too, and had several of her works produced by the famed Provincetown Players.

Category Questions

1

NATURE

1 The Furbish Louswort is a rare, fern-like snapdragon. True or false?

2 The total surface area of all the lakes and ponds in Maine is which of the following:
Ten thousand acres?
One million acres? One hundred thousand acres?

3 A hunter in Maine is legally entitled to shoot one deer with a bow and arrow, and another one with a gun. True or false?

4 What Maine fish is nicknamed "Mr. Silversides?"

5 On occasion, the clam flats along portions of the Maine coast have been forced to close because of the invasion of poisonous algae. By what name is this disastrous condition known?

6 Identify the following animal:
"I am Maine's largest bird of prey with a wing span of seven feet."
"I am primarily a scavenger." "It is illegal to shoot me."

7 Prior to the 1980 open hunting season on moose in Maine, when was the last previous moose hunting season: In 1975? In 1952? In 1935?

8 Great masses of the great-spangled fritillary invaded Maine at the turn of the century. But for some reason, they did not find the state to their liking because not one has been seen in Maine for the last fifty years. What is the great spangled fritillary?

Answers to Category Questions

1 True.

This unique plant was once believed to be endangered by the proposed Dickey-Lincoln hydroelectric project; however, populations of it have been found elsewhere. Congress has deauthorized this large dam project on the St. John River, although a proposal for a smaller dam at Lincoln School is still extant. The plant was named for Kate Furbish, a pioneer Maine botanist.

2 One million.

Maine has 2,500 lakes and ponds. The largest is Moosehead and the second largest Sebago.

3 False.

A hunter in Maine can only shoot one deer during a season. Although there are separate seasons for bows and arrows and antique muzzleloaders, tagging a deer then precludes any other hunting for deer.

4 The land-locked salmon.

Since 1969, this beautiful game fish has been the official State of Maine fish. Lake Sebago was its original home in Maine.

5 Red tide.

Because clams and mussels are siphon feeders, they take in this algae, so-named because of its rust color, and concentrate it in poisonous quantities within their bodies. Cooking does not destroy the poison, which can cause permanent paralysis in humans.

6 The bald eagle.

7 1935.

In November 1983, Maine voters decided in a referendum vote to continue the present open season on moose, initiated by the Legislature in 1980. Under this system a lottery is held and 1,000 moose hunting licenses are given out each year. It is estimated that Maine's moose herd is over 20,000.

8 A type of butterfly.

Category Questions
1
BUSINESS

9 Only one company in the nation manufactures the black field boots worn by Erik Estrada in the television series, "Chips." The boots are made by R. M. Mar-key Footwear, a company that has been in operation in what Maine community since 1975?

10 Eben Jordan was born on a farm in Danville, Maine in the year 1822. At the age of 14, he left Maine with three dollars in his pocket and later founded in Boston what famous firm?

11 In commercial fishing, which Maine county had the largest landings of fish using 1979 figures?

12 Prior to the development of chemicals, the tanning of leather was a major industry in Maine. What tree was essential in the tanning of leather before the introduction of chemicals?

13 Ice harvesting was once big business in Maine. What river was considered to yield the best ice?

14 "Flakes" were essential to the curing of fish. Were "flakes":
Chunks of salt laid over fish.
Wooden frames on which fish were carefully cured?
Bits of marsh hay that covered the fish until they were shipped?

15 How did the Canal Bank of Portland get its name?

16 The Pilgrims set up a trading post on the Kennebec River hoping that their business enterprise would help pay the many debts accumulated during their migration. What type of business was it?

9 Gardiner.

R. M. Mar-key Footwear is located in Gardiner. Incidentally, the firm also made the field boots worn by Angie Dickinson in the movie, "Dressed To Kill." A precedent for Maine-booted celebrities was perhaps established in 1927 when Charles Lindbergh flew on his historic non-stop flight to Paris wearing boots made by the G. H. Bass Company of Wilton.

10 The Jordan Marsh Company.

The Jordan Marsh department store has now spread out within New England and includes a location in the Maine Mall in South Portland.

11 Cumberland County.

Cumberland County posted the greatest haul of fish, 67,777,108 pounds, followed by Knox County with 59,554,200 pounds and Washington County with 40,302,523 pounds. The 1979 total of 232,282,582 showed a significant improvement from the all-time low of 138,359,242 in 1975. This improvement has been credited in part to the imposition of the 200-mile limit.

12 Hemlock.

Maine has large supplies of hemlock, an evergreen. The Indians made a tea from its leaves that contained Vitamin C and thus allowed them to avoid the disease of scurvy.

13 The Kennebec River.

14 Wooden frames on which fish were carefully cured.

Long before any settlements were built on the mainland, the coastal islands of Maine were visited by fishermen from Europe who set up their "flakes" for drying the abundant supplies of fish they caught and transported back across the Atlantic.

15 It was chartered to finance the construction of a waterway from Sebago Lake to the Atlantic Ocean.

16 The fur business.

The Pilgrims' earliest trading post was at Cushnoc (now Augusta) and later they tried to trade at other points in Maine, such as Pentagoet (now Castine). The trading post at Cushnoc was the scene of Maine's first recorded murder. A free-lance trapper named Hocking moved into the area and when ordered out by the Pilgrim traders, he resisted and had his head blown off. Implicated in the crime was the famous John Alden, as well as his equally famous sidekick Miles Standish. They were both, however, exonerated.

Category Questions

1

LAW

17 According to Maine's first constitution, anyone twenty-one years of age or older who was an American citizen and had been a resident of the State of Maine for at least three months, was entitled to vote. Is this true?

18 Name the only place in Maine that imposes its own season on the taking of lobsters.

19 Maine's only law school is located in a community that was once nicknamed the "Forest City." Where is the University of Maine Law School?

20 It is illegal for a deer hunter to shine a light into the deer's eyes to hypnotize it and make the deer an easy prey. What is the term for this unlawful and unsporting action?

21 You live in a Maine town that has a population of about 8,500 residents. Is your town large enough to become a city?

22 During the first decade of this century, a great number of out-of-staters built palatial homes on Mount Desert Island. Their desire to prevent a pollution problem resulted in the passage of a law that banned a particular means of transportation from the island. What did the ban prohibit?

23 Augusta attorney Melville Weston Fuller was appointed to an important national judicial post in 1888. He served in this post until 1910. What was his important position?

24 What is the term of office for a State Supreme Judicial Court Justice in Maine?

Answers to Category Questions

17 No.

It is true of men, but women were not granted the right to vote for the first hundred years of Maine's statehood. In 1920, the Maine Legislature, after a heated debate in which opponents cited the many perils of allowing women to vote, ratified the 19th Amendment to the U.S. Constitution. Neal Dow, better known in Maine for his championship of prohibition laws, was one of the early supporters of woman's suffrage.

18 Monhegan Island.

Lobstermen there have imposed a six month season on themselves. They can take lobsters from January to June.

The Monhegan lobstermen police their own activities and set their own schedules. It is said that if one of them, because of illness, cannot start the season with the others, they'll wait for him.

19 Portland.

The University of Maine Law School was opened in 1962, having been merged with Portland Law School the preceding year. It has quickly acquired a reputation for excellence, thanks to its faculty and library facilities.

20 "Jacking a deer."

21 Population has nothing to do with it.

For a town to become a city, it must simply initiate a request to the Legislature, which then passes an act of incorporation. There are no special requirements. In 1970, 36 percent of Maine people lived in the state's 22 cities. By 1980, the percentage had dropped to 31 percent.

22 The use of automobiles.

23 Chief Justice of the United States.

President Grover Cleveland appointed Fuller, a prominent Democratic activist, to head up the Supreme Court of the United States and he fulfilled the office for the rest of his life. While serving as chief justice, Fuller also helped to settle the Venezuela Boundary Dispute and from 1900–1910 was on the Permanent Court of Arbitration at the Hague (the World Court).

24 Seven years.

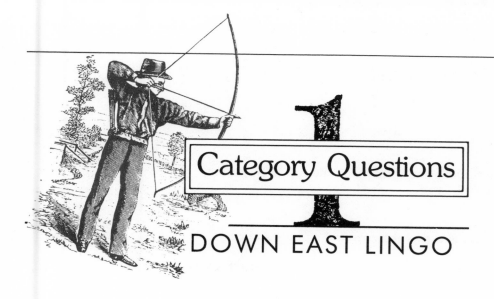

Category Questions

1

DOWN EAST LINGO

25 Men of what profession originated the term "Down East?"

26 Long before football became a major sport, Mainers were using "punts." What is a "punt?"

27 When a lobsterman talks about the "warp" of his traps, he doesn't mean they are bent or twisted. What is the "warp" of a lobster trap?

28 A "shagimaw" and a "sidehill winder" are both capable of perplexing an out-of-state hunter. In general terms, what are they?

29 Out west, a cowboy is sometimes called a "cow puncher." Who are called "cow punchers" in the State of Maine?

30 If you describe your neighbor as a kind of man who "skims his milk at both ends," do you mean that he is efficient . . . a hard worker . . . or stingy?

31 In Maine, what is an area like if it is referred to as "hard-scrabble?"

32 In the fishing industry, what is a "barvel?"

33 What is a "twitch road?"

34 Which of these three Down East terms does not necessarily refer to food?
  "Burgoo?" "Succotash?" "French toast?"

25 Sailors.

Because the prevailing winds along the coast made the trip from Boston to Maine the easy, or "downhill," run.

26 A blunt-nosed boat.

Almost rectangular in shape, it is used to row around harbors and coves.

27 The "warp" is the rope that connects the trap to the surface buoy.

28 Names of mythological animals used to fool out-of-staters.

A "shagimaw" is supposed to be a cross between a moose and a bear and a "sidehill winder" is a creature whose legs are shorter on one side because it lives on mountain slopes.

29 Veterinarians.

They got this nickname from their practice of punching cows in their stomachs to release trapped gas caused by eating fermented grain or apples.

30 Stingy.

31 An extremely rocky area, difficult to farm.

32 A leather apron.

Fishermen wear such leather aprons when they are salting down fish.

33 It is a winding road that snakes through the woods over which timber is dragged.

34 "French toast."

It refers to any silly complaint. The term derives from an attempt to unionize lumberjacks. The only thing they could think of to complain about was that they didn't get enough French toast.

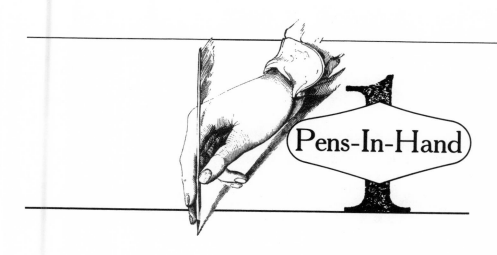

Pens-In-Hand

(a numbers game, you may want a pad for figuring)

1 In 1970, Maine celebrated its Sesquicentennial anniversary as a state. How many years of statehood was Maine celebrating in 1970?

2 How does Maine rank in size among all the other states?

3 How many towns are there in Maine?

4 How long is the Allagash Wilderness Waterway?

5 Casco Bay extends from Cape Elizabeth to the Kennebec River. It is twelve miles wide. How long is it?

6 For how many years was Prohibition in effect in Maine?

7 In 1820, Maine's population was 298,335. What was the population in 1850?

8 U.S. Route 1 originates in Florida and terminates in Maine. Altogether, how many states does it pass through?

P.S. Whoever comes closest to the correct number wins.

Answers to Pens-In-Hand

1 150 years.

Maine became a state in 1820. Its initial incorporation into Massachusetts, then a *province*, took place in 1652. After the Revolution, the first agitation for an independent Maine occurred in 1785. Six separate votes had to be taken before Massachusetts would agree to let Maine go. They did so for one major political reason: Massachusetts was a Federalist state and Maine usually voted for the opposite party — the Democrat-Republican. The move for statehood was encouraged greatly by Massachusetts' failure to protect the "District of Maine" during the War of 1812. Maine entered the Union as a free state —- along with Missouri as a slave state — in what became known as "the Missouri Compromise."

2 39th.

3 430.

In addition, there are 22 cities, 46 plantations and 41 unorganized townships.

4 92 miles.

The Allagash Wilderness Waterway runs between Aroostook County and Piscataquis County and it borders a portion of the eastern boundary of Somerset County. For a mile on each side of the Allagash River, there is a protection zone, ceded by former landowners, although the state, which controls the Waterway, only exercises complete control within a 250-foot strip on either bank. It is a favorite area for canoe trips and was established by the voters of Maine as a Waterway in 1966.

5 20 miles long.

Casco Bay is one of Maine's most important bodies of water, forming the entrance to Portland Harbor. It contains a number of inhabited islands, especially Peaks Island, from which people commute to work in Maine's largest city. A Casco Bay Ferry serves these islands.

6 83 years.

It was established in Maine in 1851 through the leadership of Neal Dow, a Civil War general who also served as mayor of Portland. Prohibition in the United States was originally known as the "Maine Law."

7 583,169.

By 1900, it had risen to 694,466, grew to 913,774 in 1950, and only broke the one million mark in 1980 with 1,123,560.

8 14.

Visual Questions

1 The call letters of Channel 10 are WCBB, standing for the three private colleges that sponsor Maine's pioneer public television station. Below are pictures of the three campuses. Identify them.

c.

a.

b.

2 Pictured in this portrait is a 19th century congressman from Maine. He was a classmate of Nathaniel Hawthorne and Franklin Pierce at Bowdoin College. He was killed in a duel with another congressman. Name him.

3 Three of Maine's historic forts are pictured here: one from the north, one from the south and one from the center of the state. Identify them, with their correct geographical locations.

a.

b.

c.

Answers to Visual Questions

1 a. Bates, b. Bowdoin, c. Colby.

Bates College in Lewiston was founded in 1855. It is named for Benjamin E. Bates, a Boston manufacturer. The current enrollment is 1,500. Edmund S. Muskie, U.S. Senator from Maine from 1958–1980, and former Secretary of State is a Bates graduate.

Colby College in Waterville was founded in 1813. It was named for Gardner Colby, a Boston merchant. The current enrollment is 1,385.

Bowdoin College in Brunswick was found in 1794. It is named for James Bowdoin, a Revolutionary War governor of Massachusetts. The current enrollment is 1,385. Among its distinguished alumni are Nathaniel Hawthorne and President Franklin Pierce. Both current U.S. Senators from Maine, William S. Cohen and George J. Mitchell, are graduates of Bowdoin.

2 Jonathan Cilley.

Cilley's death in 1838 at the hands of Congressman William Graves of Kentucky led to an outcry for the end to dueling in Washington, D.C. The move for reform was led by Cilley's fellow Maine congressman, John Fairfield of Saco, later to be governor of Maine. Ironically, Cilley was only more or less a bystander to the quarrel that eventually led to the fatal rifle exchange between himself and Graves.

John Fairfield

3 a. Fort Kent (north), b. Fort McClary (south), c. Fort Western (center).

Fort Kent

Visual Questions

4 The ship pictured here was the first vessel ever built in America. The date was 1607 and it was constructed by members of the ill-fated Popham colony. What was the name of the ship?

5 Maine's State house, pictured here, is a handsome building that has undergone extensive renovation since it was built. In what year was it completed and who was the architect?

6 Below are three of Maine's most distinctive lighthouses: one from the northern part of the state, one from the south and one closer to the center. Name them and their geographic locations.

a.

b.

c.

4 The "Virginia".

Maine's first English-speaking colony was planted in 1607, three years after the French attempted a settlement at St. Croix Island. Sent over by Sir John Popham, Lord Chief Justice of England, and Sir Ferdinando Gorges, the 120 men suffered through one of the worst winters on record and many died before they decided to abandon the place. The "Virginia" was a "pretty Pynnace" of about 30 tons and she made it back to England with a cargo of furs and sassafras roots. For 20 years, she went back and forth between England and Virginia until she was sunk off the Irish coast.

Popham Beach

5 1832; Charles Bulfinch.

The architect Charles Bulfinch also designed the Massachusetts State House and a good part of the Capitol in Washington, D.C. One of the great architects of his time, he was also for 19 years the chairman of the Board of Selectmen of Boston (then still a town, governmentally) and, in effect, its mayor.

Another View of the State House

6 a. Nubble Light, south (York Beach), b. West Quoddy Head Light, north (Lubec), c. Portland Head Light, center (Cape Elizabeth).

Essay Questions
1

THE MAINE INDIANS

Maine has been populated a long time — since 3,000 B.C., some experts say. The earliest of the Indian inhabitants were called "Red Paint People" because they lined the graves of their dead with a type of red clay. It was dug from a pit on the side of Mount Katahdin. About a thousand years ago, these early inhabitants were carving figures on the basaltic rocks of Machias Bay. These rock carvings, called Petroglyphs, are now the object of study by the Maine State Museum.

When the Vikings landed on the Maine coast about 1000 A.D., they fought with the Indians whom they called "Skralings" (which means "wretches" in old Norse).

The English settlers arrived in the 1630's and were on friendly terms with the Maine Indians until 1675, when King Philip's War spread to Maine. For the next 70 years, intermittent warfare continued, mostly as part of the struggle between France and England for control of North America. The French were always closely allied with the Maine Indians. French Jesuit priests converted many of them to Catholicism.

Maine Indians belong to the Algonquian language family. They have been classified into three separate divisions: the Abanakis (which include tribes like the Sokokis, Wawenocks, Norridgewocks, etc.), and Penobscots and the Etchemins (which include the Passamaquoddies and Malecites).

The Penobscots and the Passamaquoddies are the two major tribes remaining in Maine. The rest were exterminated or fled to Canada. Because of their aid to the Americans during the Revolution, these two tribes were allowed to stay but most of their land was taken from them by treaty.

In 1977, the two tribes, along with a small group of Malecites from Houlton, sued the State of Maine, claiming their treaties were null and void because they had never been ratified by the U.S. Congress under the Non-Intercourse Act of 1790. The Federal government supported the Maine Indians' case. In 1980, a settlement was reached for the sum of $81.5 million. The Indians' claim originally had been for $25 billion and had covered 12.5 million acres of land. The tribes are now using the money to buy land and for business investments, which include the recent purchase of a cement plant in Thomaston by the Passamaquoddies.

Big Thunder, a Penobscot, dressed as an ancient Abanaki Chief.

1. *What did the Vikings call Indians and what did it mean?*

2. *How many acres did Maine Indians claim under the Indian Land Claims Dispute?*

3. *When did King Philip's War occur?*

4. *Name two tribes who are classified as Etchemins.*

5. *What are petroglyphs?*

The sculpture of Glooskap, the mythical Abanaki deity, recently erected at Bar Harbor, shown during the installation ceremonies.

1. **Skralings. Wretches.**

2. **12.5 million.**

3. **1675.**

4. **Passamaquoddies. Malecites.**

5. **Rock carvings.**

Governor James B. Longley (in office, 1974–78), Maine's only independent governor.

A view of the Second School House at Paris Hill that existed 1800–1896.

GREENWOOD'S
"CHAMPION"
EAR PROTECTORS!

The BEST ARTICLES in the World to KEEP THE EARS WARM in the Coldest Weather. Patented in the United States and Canada.

They Fold so as to be Conveniently Carried in the Vest Pocket.

They will Wear for Years! They Sell for a Low Price!

THEY ARE WORN EXTENSIVELY BY LADIES!

They Give Universal Satisfaction wherever they have been Introduced! Over 100,000 actually worn in the United States!

For those who wish a "tony" article, we have them covered with Silk-Velvet and Satin, with Gold and Silver Plated Springs, that are just Elegant.

CHESTER GREENWOOD, Patentee and Manuf'r,

WEST FARMINGTON, MAINE, U. S. A.

Advertisement for the famed ear muffs invented by Chester Greenwood of Farmington.

Montpelier — the restored home in Thomaston of General Henry Knox, America's first Secretary of War.

Portrait of James G. Blaine, U.S. senator, secretary of state and presidential candidate.

James G. Blaine's study as it looked when he occupied the Blaine House, now the residence of Maine's governors.

A lobster's carapace, as
indicated by the arrow.

The great seal of the State of
Maine, showing the North
Star.

The sign marking the
northern terminus of U.S.
Route 1.

What You Ought to Know About Maine

HISTORY

Maine's history is rich and varied. It is a "quiet place" today, but it has been the site of warfare, whether the sudden violence of an Indian raid or the shattering bombardment of a British naval squadron. The French and the English fought over Maine. The Dutch even briefly invaded. Spanish, Portuguese and Italian adventurers, sailing under various flags, explored its coast where 600 years before parties of Norsemen had reputedly camped. The native Indians had already been there for a long, long time, and had even known an age when the climate was far warmer and drier than it is now. They hunted and farmed, and manured their crops with small herrings they called *menhaden* (meaning "they manure" in their language) and they went to the seashore in the summers and ate vast quantities of seafood, leaving great shell heaps at places like Damariscotta.

In 1979, researchers at the Maine State Museum brought a moment of Maine's pre-history to life when they positively identified a piece of coin found at Blue Hill as a genuine Norse coin. Judged to be more than 900 years old, it is the oldest known European artifact ever found in North America.

Modern history in Maine begins with the arrival of later Europeans. The French came first, and within three years, the English arrived. It was in 1604 that the nobleman, Pierre du Guast, Sieur de Monts, landed a group of settlers on an island in the St. Croix River, today's boundary between Maine and New Brunswick. Priests with the group celebrated the first Christmas Mass in this part of the New World. Although the Frenchmen weathered the winter, they moved on to better quarters (in Nova Scotia) the next spring. The Englishmen who came to Popham Beach in 1607 were not as fortunate. The winter was one of the worst in memory, many died and the whole enterprise was promptly abandoned, but not before they, too, had scored a "first": the first shipbuilding effort in North America — the construction of the "Virginia," a useful cargo vessel of 30 tons.

Five Maine Indians, kidnapped from what is now the town of St. George and brought to England by Captain George Waymouth, played a role in the further exploration of Maine. Some of them lived with Sir Ferdinando Gorges and excited in his interest in the colonizing of the bountiful territory they described. Another Maine Indian who was kidnapped and also learned English was Tisquantum, a local *sachem* or chief. As "Squanto," he has been immortalized for the help he gave to the Pilgrims during their first year at Plymouth.

The Viking coin, found at Blue Hill and identified in 1979, said to be the earliest artifact of European settlement ever discovered in North America.

Maine was good to the Pilgrims in other ways, too. They were able to pay back the financial supporters of their enterprise through the fur trading stations they established in Maine. The primary one was at Cushnoc (now Augusta) but they also had trading posts at Castine and Machias. Their insistence on a monopoly of beaver and other pelts led them into conflict with the Puritan rulers of the Massachusetts Bay Company. A sense of distinction between Massachusetts Bay and the Pilgrims at Plymouth eventually led to the absorption of Plymouth into the larger colony. Meanwhile, this Massachusetts "imperialism" also extended to Maine.

In 1652, Massachusetts commissioners came to Kittery, York and Wells and succeeded in winning the submission of the residents. Until 1820, Maine would remain under its powerful neighbor's jurisdiction.

Governed from Boston, Maine was a frontier "District." Its inhabitants, who formed the first line of defense against the French in the north, were even forbidden by a legislative act from deserting their homes. Alone, they bore the brunt of constant attacks by the Indians, who were spurred on by Frenchmen living among them, including a number of priests.

The French claim extended to the Kennebec. They did not bring settlers en masse into Maine (except in what is now northern Aroostook County) but they had strongholds where individuals like the Jesuit Father Rasle at Norridgewock or the Baron St. Castin at Pentagoet (Castine) had settled among the local tribes.

The fighting flared intermittently until the 1720's. In two important battles, at Lovewell's Pond near Fryeburg and at Norridgewock, the Indian strength was shattered by tough Maine rangers. Some of the tribes began an exodus to Canada, or farther downeast, to escape the expanding English.

In 1745 came the expedition by troops from all over New England, but especially Maine, to capture the powerful French fortress of Louisbourg on Cape Breton Island. Capture it they did, under the leadership of the Maine-born and bred wealthy merchant, William Pepperrell, who for his exploits became the first American ever ennobled by the British Crown.

Three years later the government in London handed Louisbourg back to the French for political reasons. The resentment that spread throughout New England was a forerunner of the ill-feeling against the mother country that led to the Revolution.

Maine's role in the War of Independence was not a large one. Yet battles were fought here. The very first naval battle of the conflict occurred off Machias when local fishermen, poorly armed but doughty and determined, captured a British Navy sloop, the "Margaretta." Portland was bombarded and almost totally wrecked by the vindictive Captain Henry Mowat. Benedict Arnold marched through Maine on his ill-fated mission to besiege Quebec. Castine was captured by the British and the Americans suffered a humiliating and needless naval disaster in the Penobscot River while trying to recapture it. And, of course, the Maine men fought everywhere with Washington's armies. Even the Maine Indians helped the American patriots.

With independence for the nation, independence for Maine from Massachusetts was not far off. Agitation for statehood commenced in 1785 with an article in the Falmouth (Portland) "Gazette." The first referendum vote was in 1792. Statehood lost, by a tally of 2,525 to 2,074. But again and again, the question was put before the people. The War of 1812, when Massachusetts was perceived as having done nothing to protect Maine against a British invasion of the downeast coast, fanned the flames of the breakaway movement. Finally, in 1818, a margin of 17,091 to 7,132 in favor of separation seemed overwhelming enough to persuade Massachusetts to let Maine go.

To persuade Congress to allow Maine to join the Union was still another matter. It was finally worked out in an agreement between free-soilers and pro-slavers; Maine came in as a free state; Missouri as a slave state. On March 15, 1820, Maine took its place as the 23rd of the United States of America.

Maine now had its own governor, William King of Bath, its own constitution, whose education portion had been written by Thomas Jefferson at the request of his friend Governor King, its own great seal designed by Dr. Benjamin Vaughan of Hallowell, its state flag and all other appurtenances of power. The first capitol was located in a court building erected on the site of an old stable in Portland, but by 1831 it had been removed to the handsome, grey granite, State House in Augusta — not without a struggle, however, and a running fight with Portland that lasted even into the 20th century.

A more serious dispute involved the northern boundary of the state. The Peace Treaty of 1783 had never exactly clarified where Canada ended and the United States began. Men from Maine and men from New Brunswick began to clash with each other over land and timber rights in the St. John Valley area. John Baker was arrested and carted off to a Fredericton jail for displaying an American flag. The governor of Maine threatened war. The English threatened war. Washington sent troops up into the Aroostook wilderness. But the "War" proved bloodless; diplomacy settled the boundaries through the Webster-Ashburton Treaty of 1842. A disgruntled Maine, feeling it should have had more land, reluctantly accepted what have remained its territorial limits to this day.

The next big issues to embroil the state were slavery and prohibition. Their hold on the people of Maine was to lead to a political re-alignment. Until the 1850's, Maine had been firmly in the camp of the party of Thomas Jefferson and Andrew Jackson — in other words, the Democrats. But the anti-slavery, anti-wet sentiments of the new party that formed nationally for the election of 1856 — the Republicans — changed all that. Already, by 1851, the "Maine Law," the nation's first ban on the consumption of liquor, had been passed. The Republicans won the governorship in 1856 and they were to remain in almost unbroken power for the next hundred years.

The Civil War found Maine taking an active role to defend the Union. More than 73,000 men from Maine served in the northern armies. The hero of the most critical phase of the most critical battle of the war — the defense of Little Round Top at Gettysburg — was a Maine-born general and Bowdoin professor, Joshua Chamberlain. General Chamberlain was also chosen by Grant to receive Lee's sword in surrender at Appomattox. Another Maine general, O. O. Howard, later led the Freedmen's Bureau during Reconstruction, attempting to help the freed slaves and leaving his name to posterity in Howard University. Lincoln's first vice president was another Maine man, Hannibal Hamlin. And "the little lady who started the big war," as Lincoln called her — Harriet Beecher Stowe — wrote her powerful anti-slavery novel, *Uncle Tom's Cabin*, while living in Brunswick, Maine.

The post-war period saw a strong development of industry in Maine. Into the cities, especially Lewiston and Biddeford, poured immigrants from French Canada to work in the new textile mills springing up. Irish and Italian immigrants flocked to Portland and Bangor. The logging and lumbering industry in the northern part of the state achieved near legendary status as it grew. In 1868, the pulp and paper industry began and soon expanded. By 1870, tourists were also starting to arrive. The present-day pattern of economic activity had been more or less unconsciously set.

Thus too, began a public dialogue that Mainers characterize with the phrase "payrolls or pickerels" — signifying the necessary balance that the state seeks between industry and environmental quality. It has been a constant theme in Maine over the years.

In the 1920's, Governor Percival Baxter led his own personal crusade for the preservation of the Mount Katahdin area. Unsuccessful politically, he used his own money to buy the land and donated it to the state, creating the largest state park in the country. Already, in 1919, the first national park east of the Mississippi had been established at Bar Harbor — Acadia National Park — through the leadership of such influential summer residents as John D. Rockefeller and President Charles Eliot of Harvard.

Maine's motto of "Dirigo" — "I lead" — had even more of an application than just the passage of groundbreaking laws or the creation of innovative institutions. Maine literally led the country in voting — because the state held its elections in September, not November. Thus, the popular saying, "As Maine goes, so goes the nation." In 1936, this slogan received a new twist when only staunchly G.O.P. Maine and Vermont withstood Franklin Delano Roosevelt's Democratic landslide of that year. Now we had, "As Maine goes, so goes Vermont."

In 1960, incidentally, this election law was changed and Maine finally went along with the rest of the United States. There were other changes of governmental structure to follow: a four-year term for governor (1957), a major reorganization of state government agencies (1971), abolition of the Executive Council (1975), annual sessions of the Legislature (1975).

It was in the 1970's, too, that Maine again led the nation when its Legislature passed two landmark pieces of environmental legislation, the Site Selection Law, regulating large-scale industrial projects, and the Oil Conveyance Fund Law, guarding against major oil spills. The epoch saw many environmental bills come to fruition in a movement that had grown significantly since the days of Percival Baxter's lonely fight for environmental quality.

Nuclear power also became an issue and Maine voters were the first in the nation to decide if an existing nuclear plant should be closed. On two occasions, the majority said no, by percentages of 60 to 40 and 56 to 44.

The Indian Land Claims controversy that erupted in 1977 constituted one of the most momentous challenges that the state has ever had to face. At stake was no less than two-thirds of the land area of Maine. The monetary value of the Indians' claim was $25 billion. Had the case been pressed, the Justice Department of the United States would have repre-

President Jimmy Carter signs the Maine Indian Land Claims Settlement, using a quill pen.

sented the Passamaquoddy, Penobscot and Malecite tribes who maintained that the treaties by which they had surrendered all of this land in the 18th century were in violation of a Congressional Act of 1790 and therefore null and void. The claim was settled in 1980 for $81.5 million.

Modern Maine has changed a good deal, if in nothing else than the fact that it is growing. Out-migration has slowed and the net gain of population has dramatically increased as people — many of them young — continue to flee the urban areas of the country and come to Maine. In 1971, Maine went over the one million mark and the population is still climbing far more quickly than it ever did in the past: 1,038,629 in 1973; 1,071,380 in 1976; and 1,105,000 in 1979. The future projections for all of northern New England are high and Maine, it is estimated, will increase the number of its inhabitants by 16 percent by the year 2000.

Yet modernize as it will, drawing in high-tech industries, expanding old ones in new directions like the Bath Iron Works drydock project in Portland harbor, building a stunning new art museum that attracts national attention, Maine keeps its

The Old Gaol in York, the oldest public building in the English-speaking part of North America.

values also. Humor, kindliness, good sense and, actually, a love of talk and friendly banter are hallmarks of the Maine character. As the 21st century approaches, the Maine mystique yet beckons, updated and perhaps glossier, but an invaluable, intangible asset for the Pine Tree State.

What You Ought to Know About Maine

FOLKLORE

Maine folklore begins with the Indians. A mythology as complex and imaginative as that of ancient Greece is part of the tribal tradition of the Penobscots and Passamaquoddies and other Algonquian speakers who have inhabited the state. The leading figure in this story-telling, fanciful world view is the hero-god Glooskap (there are dozens of spellings of the name). Around his central character, a whole pantheon of fabled companions exist: Poksinquis, his grandmother; Mikumwesu, the dwarf; Culloo, the giant bird; Uncle Turtle; Lex the puckish devil; and Snowy Owl who killed woolly mammoths.

Reference to Glooskap explained many natural phenomena to the Indians. Frogs are the size they are and have bends in their backs because Oglebamu, the giant frog, had swallowed all of the world's water and was sitting on top of Mount Katahdin while the forests wilted and animals thirsted. Glooskap ended this state of affairs by breaking the amphibian's back with a stone axe, reducing him to size and setting him in an environment that was neither wholly water nor land. Glooskap, in fact, often had trouble with outsized creatures like the giant squirrel he miniaturized to its present dimensions after it threatened to attack mankind, or the giant beaver he killed for building an environment-damaging dam.

Glooskap, according to the Maine Indians, was a spirit who never grew old and lived at the south end of the world with the loon and the wolf as his dogs. Glooskap put the "eyes" on birch-bark after a birch tree fell on him, hammering these indentations into it with his stone axe so that from then on it could see where to fall. In a more modern myth, Glooskap went across the ocean to visit the King of France (shades of

the French influence on the Maine Indians) but the King didn't treat him very well (shades, perhaps, of the English influence). The French monarch, angered at Glooskap and his grandmother, ordered them shot out of a cannon. When the artillery piece was fired, however, it exploded, killing 1,000 French soldiers but leaving Glooskap and Poksinquis unscathed. Disgusted with Europe, they sailed back to America on their "ship," a floating wooded island crewed by dozens of scampering squirrels. Now Glooskap sits up in his abode atop Mount Katahdin, making arrowheads for an eventual confrontation between the Indians and white men (shades of the Indian Lands Claim).

The Indians' effect on the whites survives in less fictional fashion through the well-known tale of Molly Ocket. She was a historical personage, reputedly a princess of the Pequot tribe, who had stayed in Maine after her people emigrated northward. In the Oxford County area where she was said to sleep in a cave under a boulder, she had the reputation of being a witch, but also a skilled herbalist with healing powers. A miller whom she cursed for driving her away soon lost his business and no mill has ever been able to prosper at the site. But her most enduring exploit was to minister to an ailing baby and, holding him in her hands, predict that someday he would be famous — a prophecy fulfilled when the infant Hannibal Hamlin grew up to be the vice president of the United States. Trap Corner, now West Paris village, is the place most associated with Molly Ockett who, like many a larger-than-life personality, was credited with having salted away a hidden treasure of gold.

Legends of buried gold are not as abundant in Maine as they are in the West Indies, but they do persevere. Stories of the buccaneers of the Spanish Main, as told in the little town of Woolwich in the late 1600's, inspired young William Phips, a humble gunsmith's son, to seek and — lo and behold — find a sunken Spanish treasure that made him wealthy and famous overnight. As Sir William Phips, he was the first American ever to receive a knighthood and to be made governor of Massachusetts.

Genuine pirates existed in Maine, too. The best known was Samuel Bellamy, who headquartered himself at Machias where he planned to establish a "Pirate Republic." Thwarted in his efforts, he was eventually hanged, but not before he had captured supposed millions in gold, gems, etc. from the rich British merchantman, "Whidaw," and had hidden them no one knows where. The banks of the Machias River have been one suggestion. But the most-worked location for a Jolly Roger hoard in the state is Casco Bay's Jewell Island. The purported hider of the lost trove there was none other than Captain Kidd himself. Through the years, some fairly bizarre efforts have been made to find Captain Kidd's Maine treasure. Once, lambs were slaughtered and their blood poured on the spot to chase away the ghosts and devils guarding the loot. Another time, a young girl was hypnotized on the island so she could guide the treasure seekers to the correct site. All in vain until — possibly — the arrival of a man with a pirate's map conferred with a local sea captain and then disappeared. His skeleton was later found in a shallow grave and the sea captain, since deceased, was pinpointed as having murdered him once he'd found the treasure. Pretty spooky stuff.

Jewell Island in Casco Bay, reputed site of Captain Kidd's buried treasure.

Spookier still, in terms of pirates, is the story of Blackbeard's bride. The young lady in question, who married the infamous swashbuckler on the Isles of Shoals, was only one of his fourteen wives. He left her there in that barren, offshore fishing community, and sailed away in his ship, the "Queen Anne's Revenge," promising to come back to her with a fortune. He never did. Her ghost still haunts the rockweed covered shores where she fruitlessly waited all her life. Clad in her flowing wedding gown, she ceaselessly scans the horizon, searching for the sails of the "Queen Anne's Revenge."

Another ghost that roams a Maine waterfront is that of the villainous Captain Kiff (not Kidd), a ship wrecker who lived on Cliff Island in Casco Bay. With a lighted lantern tied to the neck of his black stallion, Kiff would lure boats onto the rocks, plunder them and slaughter the survivors. It is alleged that people have disappeared searching for the concealed spoils of this murderous trade over which Kiff's evil spirit still stands guard.

The sea always has its weird tales. One of the eerier Maine ones concerns Michael Mitton, one of Maine's first settlers.

While out fishing one day — according to him — a merman attacked his boat. He saw a finny hand reach out of the water and grab a gunwhale of his rowboat, followed by the frightening form of a creature half-man, half-fish, trying to climb up into the boat. Grabbing a hatchet, the panic-stricken Mitton chopped off that barnacle-encrusted hand which, though severed completely, continued to maintain its grip on the boat for several hours!

Such tales of the supernatural have sprung up in all parts of Maine. Headless ghosts have a certain popularity in Aroostook County. A sawyer in a lumber mill who accidentally slipped and was decapitated by a saw blade may have been the origin. Yet a certain Maine matter-of-factness attends these northern yarns. Like the one about the man working in the woods one day, sitting on a log to rest, noticing a headless ghost next to him, then getting up and running like mad. When he felt safe finally, he stopped, caught his breath and sat down on a log again. Once more, however, he saw the ghost next to him. Wearily rising, he said to the headless phantom, "Well, my friend, here we go for another run."

Another folklore theme from the north woods concerns the "gorbey," which is the local name for the Canada jay, a large grey bird related to the blue jay but considerably bigger. Harming a gorbey is considered bad luck. Fairly tame creatures, they hang around the lumber camps and occasionally steal food. The story is told of a cook in one of these camps, a man extremely proud of his beautiful head of hair, and what happened to him after he caught a gorbey and plucked its feathers out. In brief, all of the cook's hair fell out overnight, and other stories tell of a hunter who shoots a gorbey and then severely injures his foot soon afterward.

Maine lumberjacks have to contend with more than inauspicious jay-like birds. Lurking in the woods, there is always Sock Saunders, the gremlin of the profession who makes life miserable for the men who cut down trees and move them; behind every accident, every snarled, dangerous log jam, one can trace the dire influence of this malevolent Anglo-Saxon sprite.

But many Maine folktales do not have to rely on occult happenings. They derive no doubt from incidents that actually took place. For example, the farmer who was asked to buy a raffle ticket on a horse. He did so and was soon informed that he had won the raffle. He went to collect his prize and found that it was a dead horse and that since he now owned it, he had to spend the money to have it buried.

Another story — definitely true — concerns a farming couple named Simpson who would take a load of produce to market once a week — a distance of 18 miles. All the while, as old Simpson drove his oxen, his wife walked beside him furiously knitting a pair of socks. She'd be finished by the time they reached their destination, and opportunely so, since her husband's socks by now were full of holes and he needed the new pair for the walk back.

Such human quirks have always intrigued Maine people. Folk heroes like Paul Bunyan have had an influence on Maine life, but more often it is real people like Jim Clarkson, the notable red-bearded hermit of Township 9, Range 14 who befriended animals. Stubborn Hiram Johnson of Chesuncook Lake dumped his collection of scrap iron into its depths after he had poled his raft 22 miles to town and failed to receive the offer of a fair price for his goods. John Cling, an eccentric Englishman who lived around Sullivan, always dressed in clothes made from flour bags and walked everywhere on eight-foot high stilts carrying a knapsack filled with tools, cooking pots, a tea kettle and several barking puppies. At Harpswell, the local authorities marooned John Darling on Pond Island because of his anti-social behavior and there he remained for upwards of twenty years, living in a shack he built from stray boards and broken lobster traps, eating sea gulls, decayed fish and eels, drinking brackish swamp water, and becoming so attached to his recluse life that he refused ever to leave it. York's Joseph Moody was another celebrated eccentric, more famous than the others because this 18th century pastor of the Second Congregational Church one day covered his face with a veil and never uncovered it again, and in so doing, became the subject of an enduring short story by Nathaniel Hawthorne, *The Minister's Black Veil.*

Stephen King, America's current master story teller of the macabre, is perhaps not wholly accidentally from Maine. A thread of deep and strange individuality combined with the quiet intensity of life in these northern climes shows itself in Maine writing, which often is just slightly removed from folklore. It happens, too, with humor, like in W. R. Pattangall's *Meddybemps Letters* or even in the *Bert and I* routines that feature the late Marshall Dodge.

The odd stories (or stories of oddness) and the calm, quaint jokes are endless, and so are the folk remedies and old wives tales. Squeezing the juice from green pine cones to produce a remedy for wrinkles, grinding deer horns or moose hooves into laxatives, treating an earache with warm fox wax and tying fish skins around a child's feet to cure a cold — these are practices that Maine people once took seriously. In the colonial medicine chest, you might have found pine pitch, hazelnuts, dogfish, cod bones, loon beaks and even wolf dung. Medicinal plants, with real therapeutic value would have been there too. Nature was not as far away in those times as it seems today in the age of antibiotics and CAT scanners.

Tongue in cheek, Artemus Ward touched this rich vein of Maine experience in advancing his recipe for hair tonic:

>"Take two kegs of hog's lard and boil to
>the consistency of mush.
>
>Stir in whiskey and musk, bottle tight
>and apply hot with a currycomb."

Undoubtedly, he wrote that with a good old Maine twinkle in his eye. Just as there is when some backwoodsman, even today, still tells the city slicker to watch out for a "tree squeak" in the forest or to be sure to report any "side hill winders" or "shagimaws" that might be seen.

What You Ought to Know About Maine

THE FRENCH QUEEN

Somewhere between history and folk romance lies the story of how Queen Marie Antoinette of France almost came to Maine to live a life of exile rather than perish under the guillotine. It is a true story — a "true romance," so to speak. Her would-be rescuer was a Yankee sea captain from Wiscasset named Samuel Clough. Chin-whiskered, cold-eyed, leather-faced, he was an unlikely type to be impressed by the plight of an aristocratic and spoiled lady. Some say he was only acting for money when in 1793, he agreed to rescue the Queen from her house arrest and carry her off to America. Fittingly — where a queen was concerned — his first task was to bring some of her elaborate palace furnishings aboard his ship so that the wife of Louis XVI, in her exile downeast, would feel as much at home as possible. This done — and no one knows how Clough managed to get the art work and delicate furniture and Sevres vases past the Revolutionary guards — it was time to fetch the Queen. Alas, it was too late. Before Marie Antoinette could slip away, she was seized, imprisoned in maximum security and eventually beheaded. Clough sailed quietly out of the French port where he was berthed and headed home with a cargo strange indeed for a Maine merchantman. The luxury articles were stored in his home in Wiscasset, and over the years they were finally scattered and lost. The Clough house, however, remains, later moved to a hilltop overlooking the village of Edgecomb.

Captain Clough is also credited with a far more enduring and perhaps more important contribution to Maine life. On one of his trips home from the Orient, he brought a certain type of cat. Those who know about these matters claim it was the ancester of the "coon cat," that rather unique feline breed for which Maine is justly noted.

ROUND

Toss-Up Questions

1 In 1725, Maine's colonial militia fought the Sokoki Indians in a decisive battle commemorated ever since as "Lovewell's Fight." Near what present-day Maine community did this battle take place?

2 Identify the following county.
"I became a county in 1839."
"People love to canoe in me."
"Some people think I look more like the Middle West than like New England."
"My inhabitants like to call me 'The County.'"

3 Admiral Donald MacMillan made 26 trips to the Arctic region on a sailing vessel that is included in the National Register of Historic Places. What is the name of this vessel?

4 The first experimental transatlantic television signal was sent and received via satellite from what rural Maine town?

5 Indians in early Maine had no matches or Zippo lighters for starting their fires. They used pieces of flint, which, when struck together, produced sparks that then ignited dry tinder. Of the following mineral materials, which one best describes flint?   a. Marble?   b. Granite?   c. Quartz?

6 On the surface, Edmund S. Muskie and James G. Blaine seem to have little in common. Muskie is a Democrat, noted, among other things, for his pioneer efforts in the U.S. Senate to protect the environment. Blaine was a Republican, widely known as a champion of business and industrial interests. What similarities do these two Maine politicians share?

Answers to Toss-Up Questions

1 Fryeburg.

Before Fryeburg was settled in the 1760's by General Joseph Frye, it was known as Pequawket. The Sokokis or Saco Indians had one of their major villages there. In 1725, following on the heels of the successful raid on the Norridgewock Indians the year before, John Lovewell led a band of rangers in a surprise attack on the encampment. Chief Paugus led his warriors in the fierce resistance that saw both Lovewell and Paugus killed and heavy casualties on both sides. The ultimate effect of the "Fight" was to cause the Sokokis to abandon their territory and disperse to Canada and "Down East."

2 Aroostook County.

Aroostook is Maine's largest county in area (6,450.7 square miles). It has almost four million acres of forestland, dwarfing in size the half million acres of potato farmland for which it is nationally famous. The northern section of Aroostook did not become part of the United States until more than 20 years after Maine became a state. This county has the distinction of having the lowest death rate in all of Maine; also the lowest divorce rate.

3 "The Bowdoin."

Donald Baxter MacMillan was graduated from Bowdoin College in 1898. He went on his first expedition to the North Pole in 1908 with another Bowdoin graduate, Admiral Robert Peary. More than 45 years later, he was still going to the arctic and Bowdoin College sponsored a number of his expeditions. During World War II, MacMillan was the recipient of the Congressional Medal of Honor. In 1954, he had a narrow escape in the polar regions when his ship was nearly destroyed. At that time, he was eighty years old.

4 Andover.

Located in Oxford County, Andover sprang into prominence in 1962 when the Telstar Earth Station was opened by the Bell Telephone Company for the revolutionary experiment of connecting America and Europe for TV transmission via satellite. The station is housed inside the Radome, the largest air inflated structure in the world, 161 feet high and 210 feet across. A hugh horn reflector antennae — 340 tons of steel and aluminum — works inside the Radome with the precision of a watch.

5 Quartz.

Flint is a type of quartz, usually black, brown or grey. Spectacular Mount Kineo, rising dramatically out of Moosehead Lake, is the largest known mass of flint in the world.

6 Both served as U.S. Secretary of State and both were unsuccessful seekers of their parties' presidential nominations.

7 In 1962, a best-selling woman author, trained as a zoologist, who often summered in Maine, wrote another best seller about the effect of pesticides on animal life. Her book *Silent Spring*, has had an enormous impact on the use of chemicals in the environment. Name this author.

8 Richardson, Mooselookmeguntic and Cupsuptic Lakes are all part of what chain of lakes?

9 During the last decade of the 19th century, Arthur Sewall, the great shipbuilder of Bath, foresaw the end of the demand for wooden ships. He built "The Dirigo" in 1894. What was different about this great ship?

10 The citizens who settled in a certain western Maine town decided to name their community "Norage." But a clerk in Boston, for some unknown reason, chose to *correct* the spelling and, in so doing, he named what Oxford County municipality?

11 Spring tides are particularly high tides, the highest there can be. They are so-named because they occur in the spring. Is this true or false?

12 On December 20, 1928, Postmaster Alden Pulsifer left the little town of Minot in Androscoggin County to deliver a pouch of mail to Montreal. What unusual mode of transportation did he use to get to Canada?
   a. Snowmobile?   b. Camel?   c. Dogsled?

7 Rachel Carson.

After earning a Master's Degree in Zoology from Johns Hopkins University, Rachel Carson went to work for the U.S. Fish and Wildlife Service and became chief editor of their publications. Her 1951 book, *The Sea Around Us*, became a sensational best seller. *Silent Spring*, which she wrote a decade later while she was gravely ill, led to direct governmental action to regulate insecticides and to ban the use of D.D.T. Her association with Maine is commemorated in the Rachel Carson Wildlife Refuge in southern York County. In 1981, the U.S. government issued a 17-cent stamp with her picture on it.

8 The Rangeley Lakes.

The region, first visited by explorers in 1794, includes also Kennebago Lake and, of course, Rangeley Lake, while small Saddleback Lake is somewhat obscured by better known Saddleback Mountain, one of Maine's larger ski resorts. Richardson is really three lakes, all connected, named for a Scotsman from Philadelphia. The reason why is perhaps more understandable once it's learned that the three original Indian names were Welokennebacook, Aldabendabagog and Molechunkamunk.

9 It was a steel sailing vessel.

The "Dirigo" weighed 2,845 tons and was the first of its kind built in America. Sewall was also a prominent political figure. Two years later in 1896, he was the vice presidential candidate on the Democratic ticket along with William Jennings Bryan, who was then making his first bid for president following his famous "Cross of Gold" speech. Bryan lost to William McKinley and Sewall went back to ship building.

10 Norway.

It would be tempting to think that the unknown impulse leading the anonymous Boston bureaucrat to annul the wishes of the people in Maine with a stroke of his pen was his knowledge about the nearby towns of Denmark and Sweden. However, Norway was incorporated in 1797, while Denmark became a town in 1807 and Sweden in 1813. Hannibal Hamlin and Artemus Ward both lived in Norway.

11 False.

Spring tides occur during the full moon and new moon when the earth, moon and sun are in line. This happens twice every month and has no relation to the seasons. The opposite of spring tides are called *neap* tides which occur when the sun and moon are at right angles.

12 Dogsled.

Pulsifer used an eight-foot long dogsled pulled by six eskimo dogs. He arrived in Montreal after a 25-day trip, averaging 50 miles per day. Over 90 percent of the route, there was no snow, either.

Toss-Up Questions

13 The French Acadian people who settled the St. John Valley in Aroostook County were essentially driven into exile by the British from their homes in Nova Scotia. They have maintained their French heritage and one will often hear more French than English in their communities. The names of some of their more prominent towns, however, do not reflect a French origin. Three are named for prominent American politicians: one, a Democratic president, another a Republican vice president and another a Whig governor of Maine. Identify *one* of these communities.

14 The sea parrot is a colorful inhabitant of Machias Seal Island. What is another name for the sea parrot?

15 How many brothers were there in the remarkable Washburn family of Livermore?

16 Identify the following Maine athlete.
"I was a full-blooded Penobscot Indian from Old Town."
"In college, I once hit a monstrous home run that broke a window in a far-off dormitory."
"Recently, the city of Cleveland celebrated a day in my name."

17 The black bear is the mascot of the University of Maine, the polar bear is the mascot of Bowdoin, the mule is the mascot of Colby. What animal is the mascot of Bates?

18 Lily Bay State Park is *not* one of Maine's coastal state parks. Where is it located?

13 The three towns are Van Buren, Hamlin, and Fort Kent.

Martin Van Buren, 8th President of the United States, Hannibal Hamlin, Lincoln's first vice president and Governor Edward Kent, in power during the Aroostook border dispute, were the three politicians. The Acadians are fiercely proud of their separate identity and celebrate their heritage through special festivals and settlements such as the Acadian Village in Van Buren where typical buildings of the early settlement days are preserved. There is even an Acadian flag, a French tricolor with a gold star of Notre Dame, completely different from the blue and white fleur-de-lis banner flown in Quebec.

14 The puffin.

A diving bird of the auk family, the puffin derives its nickname of sea parrot from the brilliant coloring of its large, triangular bill — yellow, blue and vermillion. An excellent swimmer, it waddles clumsily on land and is not graceful in flight. It nests in colonies in burrows or rock cavities.

15 Seven.

1. Algernon — Minister and banker.
2. Charles — Diplomat and inventor.
3. Samuel — Shipmaster.
4. Israel Jr. — U.S. Congressman and Maine Governor.
5. Elihu Benjamin — President U.S. Grant's Secretary of State.
6. Caldwallader — Governor of Wisconsin.
7. William Drew — U.S. Senator.

16 Louis Sockalexis.

Sockalexis played major league baseball in the 1890's with a professional team then called the Cleveland Nationals. Today, we know it as the Cleveland Indians, its name supposedly having been changed to honor Sockalexis. Speaking of illustrious brothers, Andrew Sockalexis, brother of Louis, was a member of the American track team at the 1912 Olympics in Stockholm.

17 The bobcat.

18 On Moosehead Lake.

Lily Bay is about 10 miles north of Greenville on the east shore of the lake. The land for the park was donated to the state by the Scott Paper Company. Another gift to the state in the same general area is the Squaw Mountain ski resort. Moosehead is Maine's largest lake, 35 miles long, 10 miles wide, and with a total area of 120 square miles.

Toss-Up Questions

19 What Portland man, often referred to as "the Father of the American Navy," helped to break the stranglehold of the Barbary pirates in the early 1800's?

20 An authentic home remedy used by Mainers to cure corns was the following: apply rattlesnake oil or mud turtle oil for a few nights at bedtime and this will eradicate them. Mud turtles are still around, but rattlesnakes have been extinct in Maine for a long time. How many years has it been since a genuine rattlesnake was sighted in Maine?

21 What Maine governor, a champion and self-appointed guardian of Maine's animals, established the first "Bird Day" and "Be Kind To Animals Week?"

22 Maine's valued "coon cats" are not descended from racoons, but from a cross between the oriental cat brought home from China by Captain Samuel Clough and the common house cat. Also highly prized in Maine are cats of three colors, black, white and orange. What are these cats called?

23 Where would you have to go to find Pamola Peak, Knife Edge and the Tableland?

24 Channel 10's call letters are WCBB. The *W* is an arbitrary letter assigned by the FCC to most broadcasting stations east of the Mississippi. The *CBB* stands for Colby, Bates and Bowdoin, the three colleges that support WCBB. Another important station in Maine is WCSH in Portland. What do the letters *C S H* stand for?

Answers to Toss-Up Questions

19 Commodore Edward Preble.

At an early age, Preble ran away from his home in Falmouth (Portland) and shipped out on a privateer during the American Revolution. Commissioned as an officer in the fledgling U.S. Navy, he was sent to command a squadron in the Mediterranean. During the Tripolitan War, which broke out when the United States refused to continue paying tribute to Tunisian pirates, Preble ordered the frigate "Philadelphia" to blockade Tripoli. When this ship ran aground, she was captured and her crew imprisoned, but Preble dispatched Stephen Decatur and a small commando unit on a daring raid to burn her. Troubles with the Barbary pirates persisted until Stephen Decatur forced them to discontinue their demands for tribute in 1815.

20 One hundred years.

There have been no *valid* reports of rattlesnake sightings in about a century. Some people have confused large milk snakes for rattlers. The coloration of these harmless reptiles vaguely resembles that of the timber rattlesnake and when cornered, they will coil and assume a striking posture and vibrate their tails. Maine, like Ireland, sports the enviable reputation of having no poisonous snakes at all.

21 Percival P. Baxter.

Governor Baxter loved all animals, domestic as well as wild. A lifelong batchelor, his constant companion in the Blaine House was one or another of a series of Irish setters, all named Gary. Baxter made headlines when he gave a dog to inmates at Thomaston State Prison, arguing that it would soften these hardened criminals. The governor drew even more headlines, and many angry rebukes, when he lowered the state and national flags in Maine to half-mast after the death of one of his setters.

22 Money cats.

These three-colored cats are apparently always female. Once, supposedly, a $1,000 reward was offered in Maine to anyone who could find a male money cat, but no one did. To Mainers, money cats are valuable (and they *do* fetch good prices) because they are considered to bring good luck.

23 You would have to go to Baxter State Park and climb Mount Katahdin.

All three of these distinct physical features are part of Maine's largest mountain, which is 5,267 feet high. A number of trails reach the summit, including the Appalachian Trail, which actually starts on Katahdin and stretches for more than 2,000 miles to Georgia. Maine Indians revered Katahdin as the abode of their great hero-god Glooskap. It came into the possession of the state in 1931 after Percival Baxter, using his personal fortune, bought it from the Great Northern Paper Company and gave it as a gift to the people of Maine, to be kept forever wild.

24 Congress Square Hotel.

Toss-Up Questions

25 "Reed's Rules of Order" are important to what group of Maine people?

26 A famous Maine man was known as the "Sultan of Bath" and later became known as "The Father of Maine" when he led the movement for separation from Massachusetts. Identify him.

27 What is being described?
   "At Perry, it is deep red."
   "At Bailey's Mistake, it is black."
   "At Jonesport, it is blazing white."

28 The Maine county containing the largest number of incorporated cities has four of them. Which county is this?

29 In a certain famous incident in Maine's past, the following curse was uttered:
   "You will soon die. Over your grave they will erect a stone. Upon that stone will appear the imprint of a leg."
   Where would you go in Maine to see whether or not this curse came to pass?

30 If you decided to take a trip from Bucksport to Bangor, which of the following rivers would take you to your destination?
   The Kennebec?
   The Androscoggin?
   The Penobscot?

25 State legislators.

"Reed's Rules" are rules of parliamentary procedure and it is fitting that they are used in Maine government for Thomas Brackett Reed, who devised them while Speaker of the House in Washington, D.C., was a Maine man. An imposing giant, well over six feet tall, Reed was considered one of the wittiest men ever to preside over the U.S. House of Representatives. He ruled with such a strong hand and sharp tongue that he was called "Czar" Reed.

26 William King.

King, of course, was the first governor of Maine. Originally from Scarborough, he went to Bath as a young man and entered the thriving shipbuilding industry in that community. Elected to the Massachusetts Legislature, he led the fight in Boston that eventually convinced the Bay State to allow Maine to separate. After serving as governor, King held a number of public jobs in and out of Maine. He was supervisor of the construction of the state capitol building in Augusta and on the national scene, was appointed by President James Monroe in 1821 to the commission that settled U.S. claims in Florida.

27 Sand.

At these Washington County locations, within a 40-mile radius, three separate beaches have distinctly different colored sands. North of Perry, there is even a place named Red Beach.

28 Kennebec County.

The four communities incorporated as cities are Augusta (population, 21,712), Hallowell (population, 2,482), Gardiner (population, 6,510) and Waterville (population, 17,748). Cumberland County, Maine's most populous county has three cities, Portland, South Portland and Westbrook. Five counties have no cities — Franklin, Lincoln, Oxford, Piscataquis and Somerset.

29 Bucksport.

The story deals with a murder and with Colonel Jonathan Buck, the founder of the town. A woman's body was discovered, hacked and mutilated, with one leg missing. Charged with the crime was a local eccentric who lived by himself in a shack on the outskirts of town. The evidence was circumstantial — only that this odd character had performed various chores for the murdered woman. In vain he pleaded his innocence before Colonel Buck, the magistrate in the case who inflexibly sentenced him to hang. Thus, the curse, and its aftermath when Colonel Buck died and on the granite face of the magnificent monument over his grave, the outline of a woman's leg appeared. Buck's outraged relatives had it removed with sand and pumice, but it reappeared. Removed again, the image once more returned. Over and over, the process was repeated, but the stain always remained and the Colonel's family gave up in despair. The mark can still be seen.

30 The Penobscot.

Toss-Up Questions

31 After the Civil War and until about 1900, large numbers of French Canadian immigrants came to Maine from Quebec Province, seeking jobs in the industries developing in the state's cities. A number of Maine cities, as a result, have a significant percentage of Franco-Americans in their populations. Name three cities that do.

32 What Maine governor, on January 1, 1975, ended the longest consecutive term of office served to date?

33 Who was the famous American general whose able skills as a diplomat kept the Aroostook War from bursting into open warfare between Great Britain and the United States? He was known to his men as "Old Fuss and Feathers."

34 During colonial times, certain pine trees more than twenty-four inches in diameter were marked with a broad arrow and confiscated by the King's agents. To what use were these trees eventually put?

35 An old Indian chief by the name of Orono died in 1801 at well over the age of 100. He is buried in Orono, Maine, and the following inscription is on his tombstone.
　　"Safe lodged within his blanket below
　　Lie the last relics of old Orono.
　　Worn down with age, he in a trice
　　Exchanged his wigwam for paradise."
Orono was chief of what Indian tribe?

Answers to Toss-Up Questions

31 These cities are Lewiston, Auburn, Biddeford, Sanford, Saco, Brunswick, Augusta, Waterville, Old Town.

32 Kenneth M. Curtis.

Maine's four-year term for governor was instituted in 1957 and the first governor to be elected for four years was a Democrat, Clinton Clauson. Republican Senate president John H. Reed of Fort Fairfield, succeeded to the governorship in 1959 upon the sudden death in office of Clausen. Reed had served a total of seven years when he was defeated by Democrat Curtis. To date, the Curtis record of eight consecutive years has not been matched although it will be when Governor Joseph E. Brennan completes his second four-year term. The Maine Constitution allows only two consecutive terms for governor.

33 General Winfield Scott.

Scott was a Virginian who distinguished himself in the War of 1812 and became a Brigadier General at the age of 28. Sent to South Carolina during the Nullification crisis by President Andrew Jackson, he first showed his diplomatic skills and brought them into play again in easing tensions along the Canadian border with the Mid-West in 1838. A year later, he was in Maine, leading Federal troops to a possible confrontation with the British in New Brunswick. Scott's talent for peacemaking helped calm things down. He was supreme commander of the U.S. forces during the Mexican War and he ran unsuccessfully for president on the Whig ticket in 1852, losing to Bowdoin graduate Franklin Pierce.

34 They became masts for the Royal Navy.

This practice caused a great deal of ill will in the American colonies. The King's agents were often harassed — sometimes legally in the courts with the connivance of local judges and sometimes they were even physically attacked. General Samuel Waldo, for whom Waldo County and Waldoboro were named, was the prime commercial agent in Maine for these pine trees. The King's Surveyor of the Woods was charged with enforcing the laws. The broad arrows, by the way, were carved with the point upward.

35 The Penobscots.

Joseph Orono was an unusual Indian in more ways than one. For example, he was blond and blue-eyed. It was suspected that he might have been a white captured as a child and raised as an Indian, although rumors also persisted that he was an illegitimate son of Baron St. Castin. Orono met with George Washington in Cambridge, Massachusetts at the start of the Revolution and supported the Americans during their struggle against the British, chiefly by having his people do intelligence work behind the British lines.

Toss-Up Questions

36 Captain John Mason owned a plantation on the banks of the Piscataqua River near the present-day town of South Berwick. In 1634, this plantation was the site of the first water-powered mill in Maine. What did the mill produce?

37 Maine potato growers want you to know that, contrary to some public opinion, potatoes are not fattening. How many calories are there in an ordinary potato baked in its skin?

38 Coburn Gore and Misery Gore are locations in northern Maine. What does the term "Gore" signify? Is it:
   A deep, sharp valley cut by a stream?
   A pie-shaped area of land?
   A steep waterfall?

39 How do you measure a lobster to determine its legal size? Is it measured:
   From the tip of its right claw to the base of its tail?
   From the eye socket to the base of the tail?
   From the tip of its antennae to the base of its tail?

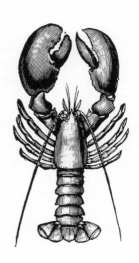

40 Another lobster question. How often does a female lobster usually lay her eggs?
   Every six months? Once a year? Once every two years?

41 Knox County, established in 1860, is Maine's youngest county. What is Maine's oldest county?

42 The largest member of the rodent family found in Maine also happens to be the largest rodent in North America. Name this sharp-toothed creature.

36 Lumber. It was a saw mill.

This saw mill was the first in America to use gang saws and their efficiency so speeded up production that the crews boasted they were performing "great works." Since then, the site in question has been called Great Works and can be visited today just on the outskirts of South Berwick.

37 93 calories.

A potato boiled in its skin has even less calories — only 76, and if the skin is removed, 65 calories. The amount here is three and one-half ounces and a comparable calorie count for the same quantity of fried bacon would be 611 calories; doughnut 391 calories; whiskey 249 calories; ice cream 207 calories. It takes 11 pounds of potatoes to produce one pound of body fat, but only three of bread, four of hamburger and one of margarine. In the United States, the per capita demand for potatoes is 118 pounds. Potatoes are Maine's largest agricultural crop. Aroostook County produces about 90 percent of them while some are also grown in Penobscot, Waldo, Somerset, Kennebec, Androscoggin and Oxford Counties.

38 A pie-shaped area of land.

These "gores" resulted from the fact that some surveyors used magnetic north and south while others used the true north and south meridians for surveying. As a result, a discrepancy occurred in the laying out of lots in the areas and pie-shaped pieces were left.

39 From the eye socket to the base of the tail.

A lobsterman carries a measuring gauge with him and if there is the slightest bit of give, the undersized crustacean has to go back overboard as a "short." There are heavy fines for keeping short lobsters. Only recently, New Hampshire has agreed to use the stricter Maine measurement of three and three-sixteenths of an inch. It takes about five years for a lobster to grow to legal size.

40 Once every two years.

When a female lobster does lay her eggs, she lays thousands at a time, but only a few of those that hatch into larvae survive. A fully gravid female has the eggs appear in large masses on her underbelly. These "eggers," when caught in traps, have their tail fins notched as a sign that they are breeding lobsters and they are then released; keeping an "egger" is strictly prohibited, as is keeping a notched lobster when the eggs aren't visible.

41 York County.

York County was created in 1652, the year of the Massachusetts takeover. Initially, it was known as Yorkshire Province. It was officially incorporated as York County in 1760. It is Maine's fastest growing county and second most populous county, having increased its population by 25 percent between 1970 and 1980.

42 The beaver.

Castor canadiensis, the North American beaver, (there is also a European species) was one of the mainstays of Maine's colonial economy.

Category Questions

2 PEOPLE

1 This legendary jack-of-all-trades and master of *all* was a resident of Blue Hill. He was a parson, architect, draftsman, tool maker, furniture maker, portrait and landscape painter, etc. — a man of extraordinary ability. Name him.

2 This distinguished Maine man was born in Leeds, became a high ranking officer during the Civil War and was a founder of a university for black people. Who was he?

3 Who was the Gardiner resident and Pulitzer Prize winning poet who wrote *Miniver Cheevy* and *Richard Cory?*

4 Identify the following person:
"I was born in Albion, Maine and was graduated from Colby College. In 1832, I began printing an anti-slavery newspaper in St. Louis, Missouri. In 1837, a mob attacked my printing office in Illinois and I was shot and killed."

5 Identify this Maine politician:
"I served in the Legislature and eventually became Chief Justice of the Maine Supreme Court. First a Republican, then a Democrat, I lampooned Maine politics in *The Meddybemps Letters.*"

6 James B. Longley was the only independent governor ever to serve in Maine. What does his middle initial stand for?

7 What was the name of the early Maine newspaper editor and publisher who wrote the satirical *Major Downing Letters*?

8 In 1799, what prominent American patriot was courtmartialed for his part in the "Penobscot Expedition," the ill-fated attempt to recapture Castine from the British?

Answers to Category Questions

1 Jonathan Fisher.

In addition to the talents already noted, Pastor Fisher (he was Blue Hill's first settled minister) was a farmer, a writer of both poetry and prose, a mathematician and surveyor, and the father of a large family. A Harvard graduate, Fisher was an active trustee of the Bangor Theological Seminary, a strong abolitionist and a founder of the American Society for the Colonization of Liberia.

2 General Oliver Otis Howard.

Left with one-arm when wounded early in the Civil War, Howard fought all through the conflict from Bull Run to Gettysburg. During the Reconstruction period, President Andrew Johnson named Howard the head of the Freedmen's Bureau, in charge of the welfare of all emancipated slaves. A founder of Howard University, he was its president for four years. As an Army commander, he later negotiated a treaty with the famous Indian, Chief Joseph.

3 Edwin Arlington Robinson.

Robinson was one of the leading poets of his time. President Theodore Roosevelt, who liked his poetry, helped him by giving him a job in the New York Customs House. In his poems, *Tilbury Town* represents the city of Gardiner where he grew up and where the Edwin Arlington Robinson House still stands.

4 Elijah Lovejoy.

Forced out of pro-slavery Missouri in 1836, Lovejoy moved to nearby Alton, Illinois. Mobs, on three occasions, destroyed his presses and then killed him when he tried to defend still another. He has been called American journalism's first martyr and every year, a journalism award in his honor is awarded by Colby College.

5 William Robinson Pattangall.

6 Bernard.

7 Seba Smith.

Seba Smith, a Bowdoin-educated schoolmaster turned newspaper editor, also owned an interest in Portland's *Eastern Argus*. In the early 1830's, after leaving the Argus to publish the *Daily Courier*, he created Major Jack Downing, a country bumpkin character who commented on political foibles. W. R. Pattangall followed in the same tradition when he wrote *The Meddybemps Letters*.

8 Paul Revere.

Revere was acquitted of the charges and he returned to his silversmithing, for which he was justly renowned. Full blame for the Penobscot fiasco was placed on the commander, Dudley Saltonstall, who *was* court-martialed. It was one of the worst defeats in American history, with the loss of almost 40 ships and 500 American lives.

Category Questions

2 PLACES

9 Moosehead Lake is the second largest body of fresh water within the boundaries of one state. True or False?

10 On what island is the Governor Baxter School for the Deaf located?

11 What is the smallest Maine county in area?

12 What is the name of the mountain located in Paris, Maine that is known to rockhounds all over the country for its rich deposits of garnet, tourmaline and quartz?

13 In the 19th century, the "Devil's Half Acre" was the area favored by brawling, high-living lumbermen during "rest and recreation" breaks from their dangerous jobs. In what city was this equally dangerous "Devil's Half Acre" located?

14 In 1820, Portland was Maine's largest community. Which of the following was the second largest?
   Bath? North Yarmouth? Lewiston? Bangor?

15 Gadabout Gaddis Airport, named for the famous fisherman, lies just south of the Maine town that serious anglers consider a fine jumping-off spot enroute to some of the area's great fishing waters. Where is the airport?

16 Beyond Alna, on Route 194, an early meeting house, a school and an 1890's store are but three of the points of interest in the beautiful little community that was the birthplace of Edwin Arlington Robinson. Name this National Historic District where the famous Maine poet was born.

Answers to Category Questions

9 False.

Moosehead Lake is the *largest* body of fresh water within the boundaries of one state. The Great Salt Lake in Utah is larger, but it's not a fresh water lake.

10 Mackworth Island.

The school is so named because the island and the funds for the construction of the school were donated to the state by former Governor Percival Baxter in 1953. The island was the site of a Baxter family summer home. Buried on the grounds in a small cemetery are the remains of the numerous Irish setter dogs that Governor Baxter owned.

11 Sagadahoc.

Sagadahoc has only 257 square miles. It is also the Maine county with the least number of farms — 108 at last count. Merrymeeting Bay, the confluence of five major Maine rivers, is in Sagadahoc and constitutes a resting place for thousands of migrating wild ducks and Canada geese. Maine's first settlement — at Popham Beach — was in this country. With a population of 28,763 in 1979, it also has the highest birth rate and divorce rate in the state.

12 Mount Mica.

The mines at Mount Mica have produced some of the finest tourmalines in the world. It has been claimed that nowhere else except Brazil can one find such an assortment of precious and semi-precious stones as in this area, including amethysts, beryls, aquamarines, garnets, rose quartz and pink, green, blue and yellow tourmalines. The biggest beryls ever found — the Havey Crystals — were discovered in this area.

13 Bangor.

The "Devil's Half Acre," notorious for its raucous taverns and houses of ill fame, has been torn down to make room for urban renewal.

14 North Yarmouth.

Today, North Yarmouth has 1,918 residents, while Portland has 61,530, Lewiston 40,534 and Bangor 31,645.

15 Bingham.

16 Head Tide.

Although Edwin Arlington Robinson was born in this small village, he grew up in Gardiner and is intimately associated with that city.

Category Questions

AGRICULTURAL AND MARINE

17 In what Maine town was the Maine State College of Agriculture and Industrial Arts established in 1865?

18 Anadama bread is acknowledged to be an original American recipe. Maine cooks believe that the recipe was created here in this state, but cooks in other states dispute this claim. Regardless of its birthplace, what two ingredients make Anadama bread unique?

19 Approximately what percent of Maine's total land area is farmland?
   22%? 13%? 9%?

20 What farm implement is pictured on the Maine State Seal?

21 What marine object is pictured on the Maine State Seal?

22 On which of the following would you find "oakum"?
   A steel vessel? A fiberglass canoe? A wooden ship?

23 If you set sail on a Friday on a ship that was painted blue, what kind of a voyage would you have?

24 Which of the following is being described? The homes of most sea-going men included one of these because they provided an excellent vantage point from which the seafarer's wife could watch for the sight of sails against the horizon.
   A spyglass?
   A widow's walk?
   A capstan?

Answers to Category Questions

17 Orono.

In time, this land grant college grew into the University of Maine. An early promoter of Maine agriculture, Dr. Ezekiel Holmes, editor of *The Maine Farmer*, which he started in 1833, helped lay the groundwork for this institution. The University now has diverse campuses — at Orono-Bangor, Portland-Gorham, Farmington, Presque Isle, Fort Kent, Machias and Augusta, and separate non-campus programs in a number of locations.

18 Cornmeal and molasses.

19 Nine percent.

Agriculture is a more than $400 million a year business in Maine. Of this value of production, the greatest single percentage surprisingly was eggs at 25 percent, followed by potatoes 21 percent and broilers 21 percent (1979 figures). There are about 7,600 farms in Maine. However, in comparison to the low amount of farmland, Maine is now 89 percent forested (the most heavily forested state in the Union). Pulp and paper, alone, is a two billion dollar a year industry in Maine.

20 A scythe.

21 An anchor.

The Maine State Seal, which bears the figures of both a farmer and a sailor, was designed by Dr. Benjamin Vaughan of Hallowell. Vaughan was an English physician and scholar who did not come to American until after the American Revolution and, indeed, he fled here from France during the French Revolution. He was a friend of many prominent people of the time, including John Adams, Benjamin Franklin, Thomas Jefferson, the Marquis de Lafayette and the Duke of Talleyrand, reputed to have been born in Maine, who visited him in Hallowell. A moose and a pine tree on the State Seal, plus the North Star, complete the symbolism.

22 A wooden ship.

Oakum is caulking used to seal seams on wooden ships. It is made from untwisted old rope.

23 Theoretically, disastrous.

Sailors are extremely superstitious. The worst possible day to begin any voyage, in their eyes, is Friday. Blue, because it is the color of the ocean, denotes to them that anything of that color will remain in the ocean: i.e. sink. Other no-no's at sea are: to have a pig aboard or even a picture of a pig; to have a cat; or to have a clergyman. The theory on the latter is that since a clergyman fights the devil, the devil might retaliate while the sky pilot is aboard. There are probably practical reasons why a pig or a cat is taboo.

24 A widow's walk.

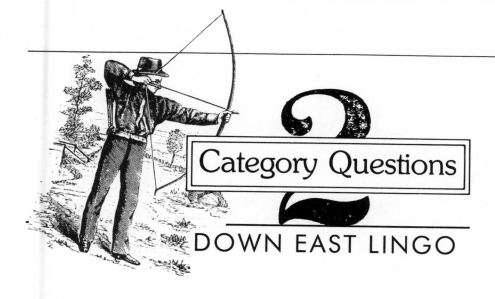

Category Questions

DOWN EAST LINGO

25 What was a "shift" or "smock" marriage?

26 Who originated the expression, "lock, stock and barrel?"

27 You are serving dessert to your guests. One guest says, "I'll take a scrid." What's a "scrid?"

28 If your neighbor told you he had just finished constructing something that was "horse high, bull proof and pig tight," what project had he completed?

29 You are said to be "on your beam ends." Are you in good shape or are you experiencing great difficulty?

30 Your grandparents may have owned a "pung." What is a "pung?"

31 When times are hard, many Maine families are served a steaming pot of "scouse." What is "scouse?"

32 Many seafood restaurants in Maine provide their patrons with "gurrybutts." What are they used for?

33 What kind of a building is an "apple knocker?"

34 Fish cleanings, particularly those that stick to clothing, gear and boats, are known as which of the following?
Scrog?
Gurry?
Scrapple?

25 Marriage to a widow without a dowry.

The term (and the practice) occurred until the beginning of the 19th century. If the lady was married naked (in a closet, of course) or in a chemise or smock, her new husband would not be responsible for any debts incurred by her previous husband.

26 Gunsmiths.

The expression originated in the workshops of those gunsmiths who made each and every part of the gun themselves. Many gunsmiths made only portions of the guns and used parts from other sources, but the gunmaker who produced his weapon "lock, stock and barrel" was greatly admired.

27 A tiny portion.

28 Building a fence.

29 You're in bad shape.

Like a shipwreck, which rests on the ends of her beams, you're a pretty sad sight yourself.

30 A box-like sleigh drawn by one horse.

31 Clam chowder made without clams.

32 Receptacles for refuse.

In a restaurant, "gurrybutts" would be containers into which to put empty clam shells and discarded lobster debris. Since "gurry" also refers to fish cleanings, on a boat it would be any barrel or bucket used to collect guts, trimmings or other such slop.

33 A privy or outhouse.

The name arose because these buildings, located out back, were often under apple trees. Occasionally, an apple would fall on the roof and disturb one's meditation.

34 Gurry.

Scrog is a weather-beaten bush by the ocean. Scrapple is a Pennsylvania Dutch breakfast concoction.

1 If you wanted to run for the Maine State Senate or any elected county office except County Commissioner in a county of less than 50,000 people, how many registered voters would have to sign your nominating petition?

2 In 1905, how much would it have cost you to get a driver's license and to register your car in the State of Maine?

3 Eastport and Lubec are separated by only three miles of water. If you wanted to travel from Eastport to Lubec by car, how many miles would you have to drive?

4 Name two of the five Maine counties that share the same names with counties in England.

5 Admiral Robert Peary is credited with being the first explorer to reach the North Pole. In what year did he accomplish this outstanding feat?

6 If it were possible to drive up Maine's coastline in a straight line from Kittery to the Canadian border, you would drive 228 miles. If you decided, however, to drive Maine's ragged coastline, taking in all the bays and inlets along the way, how many miles would it be?

7 There are three county seats in the State of Maine that begin with the letter "A." Name two of them.

8 The Maine House of Representatives is made up of how many members?

1 A minimum of 100 and a maximum of 150 registered voters.

They have to be members of your own political party and the affiliation and status of voters must be certified by the voter registrars in your district. County commissioner candidates in counties of 50,000 or less need only 50–75 names. House of Representative candidates need a minimum of 25 signatures and a maximum of 40. Independent candidates have different requirements. For the State Senate, they must have a minimum of 200 signatures and a maximum of 300. To run for county office, the figures for an Independent candidate are 300–400 names, and for the House of Representatives, 50–80 names. Their signatures must be submitted five days before the filing date of April 1, but if the office is not contested, they do not have to be put in until the primary day in June.

2 $4.00.

The fee then was $2.00 for the license and $2.00 for the registration. Today it is $18.00 for your license and $20.00 for your registration in addition to an excise tax on your automobile.

3 About 40 miles.

From Eastport, you would have to drive northwest on Route 190 to Route 1, then south on Route 1 to Route 189 and east to Lubec. Causing the problem is Cobscook Bay.

4 York, Cumberland, Somerset, Oxford, Lincoln.

In England, of course, the counties are called shires.

5 1909.

By 1909, when Peary made his epic achievement, he had already been exploring in the far north for more than 20 years. His accomplishment was later disputed by a member of one of his earlier expeditions, Dr. Frederick Cook, who claimed to have reached the Pole before him. However, Congress recognized Peary's claim. His wife Josephine accompanied him and gave birth to the first white child born north of the Arctic Circle, Marie Ahnighito Peary, who was called the "Snow Baby."

6 3,478 miles.

7 Auburn, Alfred, Augusta.

The other county seats in Maine are: Paris, Portland, Houlton, Farmington, Ellsworth, Rockland, Wiscasset, Bangor, Dover-Foxcroft, Bath, Skowhegan, Belfast and Machias.

8 151 members.

The current size of the Maine House is the result of a compromise reached at the Constitutional Convention that determined Maine's governmental structure prior to statehood. The large communities wanted a smaller legislature where their numbers would have more influence; they would have liked about 100 House members, while the small towns, with the opposite idea in mind, wanted about 400 (like New Hampshire today).

Visual Questions

1 The house pictured here is the most frequently visited historic home in Maine. It is located in Portland and was the childhood residence of one of the state's most illustrious citizens of all time. He was a Bowdoin graduate and taught at Bowdoin and at Harvard, but he was best known for his literary work. He died in 1882. What house is it?

2 The monument that is pictured at right commemorates Father Sebastian Rasle, a Jesuit priest who lived with the Indian tribes in Maine in the 18th century. He was killed during the fighting that raged when the Indian village where he resided was raided by a militia group of English settlers from the York-Kittery area. The monument is located in that same community on the banks of the Kennebec River where this incident occurred. Name the town.

3 At right is probably the most photographed signpost in the country. In addition to the names of communities in Maine that bear the same names as foreign countries or foreign cities, there are many other Maine municipalities that could also have been put on this sign. Name eight Maine communities not listed on the sign that have the same names as foreign countries, cities or towns (but do not include any in Great Britain).

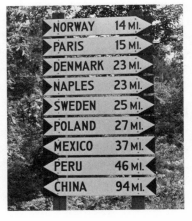

Answers to Visual Questions

1 The Wadsworth-Longfellow House.

This was the house in which Henry Wadsworth Longfellow grew up. It is owned today by the Maine Historical Society and is open as a museum. The house belonged originally to Longfellow's grandparents. His father, Stephen, a schoolteacher, later became controversial for his political stands in opposition to the War of 1812 and statehood for Maine. Longfellow was a professor of languages at Harvard. When his wife died in an accidental fire, he was badly burned trying to rescue her, and it was said that he grew his famous beard in order to hide the scars. *Evangeline*, *Hiawatha*, *The Courtship of Miles Standish* and *Paul Revere's Ride* are among the classics he wrote.

2 Norridgewock.

On August 12, 1724, Captains Jeremiah Moulton and Johnson Harmon, both of York, led their forces in a surprise attack on this stronghold of the Kennebec Indians. Rasle was apparently shot by Lt. Richard Jacques, the son-in-law of Captain Harmon. Moulton was quite angry because he wanted to capture Rasle alive and use him in a show trial to prove that the Jesuits were inciting the Indians to attack the English. In some respects, the raid was revenge for the 1692 York "massacre" in which a Protestant clergyman had been killed and Moulton's own parents slain. Rasle was a controversial figure. Some people consider him merely a saintly man whose devotion to the Indians and their spiritual needs was unexcelled and wholly peaceful.

3 Here is a full list of 24.

Athens, Belgrade, Bremen, Brunswick, Calais, Carthage, Corinth, Dresden, Embden, Frankfort, Hanover, Lebanon, Lisbon, Lubec(k), Madrid, Moscow, Palermo, Rome, Smyrna, Sorrento, Stockholm, Troy, Verona, Vienna.

Visual Questions

4 Pictured here is a unique-looking type of vessel that was used for commerce on the Piscataqua River and other waterways in southern York County during colonial days. The name for this type of vessel is an English version of the name of an Italian boat associated with Venice. What is its name?

5 Two ships are pictured here in a scene that is one of Maine's most picturesque. It was taken from the banks of the Sheepscot River in a community that calls itself "the prettiest village in Maine." Identify the community.

6 Another nautical theme. You are looking at a picture of one of Maine's most beloved and famous seafarers. Like many transients connected with the state, he summers in Maine and winters elsewhere. The governor of Maine unleashed a wave of protest when it was mistakenly believed that he had slighted him with a remark. Who is this important celebrity?

Answers to Visual Questions

4 A gundalow.

The Italian craft for which it is named is a *gondola*, the canoe-like boat that is poled through the canals of Venice. The gundalow's shallow draft allowed it to carry freight back and forth on the tidal rivers and bays of the Piscataqua region. Pictured here is a replica of a gundalow, recently built, while it was visiting the John Hancock Wharf in York.

5 Wiscasset.

These gently decaying old ships are over 200 feet long. Wiscasset claims they are the most frequently photographed objects on the Maine coast. The town also contains the Old Customs House, the Old Lincoln County Jail (Maine's first penitentiary), the Lincoln County Courthouse and the controversial Maine Yankee Atomic Power Plant.

Wiscasset County Jail

6 Andre the Seal.

From his home base in Rockport, Andre, a particularly intelligent harbor seal, now treks to the Mystic Seaport in Connecticut where he spends the winter. Then, he returns to Maine in the spring. He has been the subject of books, films and inumerable articles and is a genuine folk hero in Maine.

2 Essay Questions

THE BIRDS OF MAINE

The black-capped chickadee is the State bird of Maine and this bustling, little grey, white and black creature is familiar to everyone. Less well known is the fact that there is a *brown-capped* chickadee, a bird of the northern woods that looks very much like its southern cousin except for the color of its head.

A division between the far north and the rest of the state is one feature of the ornithology of Maine. The Canada jay or grey jay (the "gorbey") has already been mentioned. Most Mainers know only the noisy and beautiful blue jay. The grey jay, a persistent visitor to lumber camps, is credited with having saved the lives of persons lost in the forest. They merely followed one of these semi-tame creatures until it led them to a lumber camp. The tameness of another northern species — the spruce grouse — has also helped people to survive in the woods. Easily approached, the birds may be taken for food without the use of conventional weapons.

The upland game birds of Maine are primarily the ruffed grouse (called a "partridge"), the woodcock and the pheasant. The latter is at about the limit of its northern range in Maine and for some years, the state has stocked them. Duck hunting, especially of black ducks, is likewise popular. Some people also hunt sea ducks.

Along the coast, there are many species of sea birds. The herring gull is a common sight, and increasing in numbers are the larger black-backed gulls and the cormorants. Snowy egrets, once almost extinct, can now be seen in Maine marshes as can great blue herons. Innumerable sandpipers of various species and diverse wading birds inhabit the shores.

Inland, the farm country contains meadowlarks, killdeers, bobolinks and other insect feeders. Swallows, whether barn

swallows or tree swallows, are everywhere, and houses are put out in hopes of attracting those beautiful giants of the swallow clan — the purple martens.

On bodies of fresh water, the loon makes its presence known. Its crazed laughter is a haunting and nostalgic sound.

On lawns, the song sparrow or the white-throated sparrow can often be seen; the robin is always there in season; juncos and purple finches sometimes appear; and one might see a flicker, a type of woodpecker; dead trees harbor other woodpecker types, like the hairy and the downy.

New to Maine but seen with increasing frequency are immigrants from the south — the cardinal and the mockingbird.

Eagles still live in Maine — not many of them, but they are highly protected.

For bird lovers, Maine's varied avian populations provide constant and diverse entertainment.

1. *Where does the brown-capped chickadee live?*

2. *What is another name for the Canada jay?*

3. *What game bird is stocked in Maine?*

4. *What is a large swallow that nests in a special house?*

5. *What is another name for a partridge?*

A great blue heron, the large shore bird that has returned to Maine in growing numbers.

The spruce grouse of the north Maine woods.

1. **In the northern woods.**

2. **The grey jay. Also, it is called the "gorbey."**

3. **The pheasant. (technically, the ring-necked pheasant).**

4. **The purple marten.**

5. **Ruffed grouse.**

Edmund S. Muskie, Maine
governor, U.S. senator and
later secretary of state, hard
at work on a Maine lobster.

View of Mount Kineo, the
spectacular flintstone
landmark in Moosehead Lake
and the site, in the 19th.
century, of a famous hotel
and resort.

Governor Percival Baxter, portrayed with his Irish setter Gary. When the dog died, Baxter outraged many people by ordering official flags to be flown at half-mast.

Rachel Carson
USA 17c

The stamp honoring Rachel Carson, best-selling author, environmentalist and long-time Maine summer resident.

Puffins — the colorful, once-threatened sea birds now making a comeback along the Maine coast.

The Great Works in South Berwick, the site of the first water power-driven mill in Maine.

Gravestone of Colonel Jonathan Buck at Bucksport, showing the famed outline of a female leg that appeared there in fulfillment of a curse.

Mount Katahdin, Maine's highest peak. Thanks to Percival Baxter's personal generosity, it now belongs to the people of Maine.

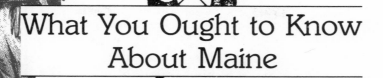

What You Ought to Know About Maine

MAINE'S CHANGING WILDLIFE

Nothing in nature is ever static. Even if left to its own devices, the natural environment will change and man's intervention merely hastens the process. Thus the picture of wildlife in Maine, as in the rest of the country, even over a period of less than two hundred years, is a fluid one.

Creatures that were familiar to the earliest settlers of Maine are now gone forever. Others that they never knew are now here. Some, like the moose that Governor James Sullivan described as "rare" in his *History of the District of Maine*, written in 1795, have had their ups and downs. They have grown in numbers, then declined, then grown plentiful again.

John Josselyn, an English naturalist living in Scarborough in the early and middle 1600's, wrote of the following animal, "There are millions of millions of them . . . so I could see no sun." Josselyn was speaking, of course, of the passenger pigeon, that prolific and doomed bird whose numbers were as great in Maine as elsewhere on the continent. Maine's role in their eventual extinction was, no doubt, minor, but Maine hunters contributed to their slaughter with the same recklessness that occurred throughout America. In 1820, the passenger pigeon was still abundant in Maine. By the middle of the century, after years of shooting and trapping, its numbers had greatly declined. The last positive record of a bird shot was at Dexter in 1896, although another may have been killed at Bar Harbor in 1904. The absolute end for this poor creature, once considered an inexhaustible resource, came in 1914 when the last one died at the Cincinnati Zoo.

The great sea mink was hunted to extinction off the coasts of Maine. It was a good-sized example of a mink, about three feet long, abundant in Penobscot Bay and northward into the Bay of Fundy. The pelt was more reddish than that of the common mink and also coarser. They were almost invariably shot or hunted with dogs, rather than trapped. Hunters carried crowbars and shovels to help dislodge the minks from cracks and holes in ledges where they took refuge. Sometimes, charges of pepper were fired in to force out the minks or brimstone fires were lit to smoke them out. Now, the sea mink is gone and there is only one known mounted specimen in existence.

The Labrador duck, which wintered in Maine, was another victim of man's heedlessness in those days before ecological consciousness was raised. The duck was smaller than an eider, which it resembled, and was killed by the millions, mostly for its feathers. The last known Labrador duck was taken off Long Island, New York, in 1875.

The great auk, sometimes called the "sea penguin," is likewise "as dead as the Dodo" (another flightless bird, long extinct). These great auks formerly inhabited Maine. About the size of a goose, black above and greyish white below, great auks were sought for their flesh, feathers and oil. By 1844, they had disappeared from the face of the earth.

Some animals, once prevalent in Maine, still exist as living species but have left the state. The most noted examples are the caribou and the wild turkey. Attempts have been made by the Maine Department of Inland Fisheries and Wildlife to return these creatures to the habitats in Maine that formerly nourished them. With the caribou, the experiment apparently has not been a success; with the wild turkey, there is evidence that their numbers are increasing although not to the point where hunting can be allowed.

Some of the creatures no longer here are definitely not missed. The timber rattlesnake is a prime example. At one time, it was found in the southern parts of Maine. An entry in the diary of the Reverend Joseph Moody written in the 1730's talks of a "three foot rattlesnake" killed in York. A story rife in western Cumberland County is that the last rattler destroyed in Maine was coiled on the steps of a church in Casco and discovered by the parishioners on their way out.

It has been about a hundred years since a valid sighting of a rattlesnake has been reported in Maine.

The timber wolf was once common here. Bounties were placed on them in 1832 and continued until 1916. Few were left by the time of the Civil War, although northern trappers feel that an occasional wolf enters the state from Canada. A wolf shot in Washington County in 1953 was believed to have escaped from a travelling zoo.

The presence of the cougar or mountain lion in Maine is occasionally still reported. The last known kill of one occurred at Mount Kineo in 1906. Game authorities feel that this panther-like big cat all but disappeared from the eastern half of the United States (except for Florida) in 1920.

Some species thought to be extinct in Maine no longer are so. A prime example is the blueback trout. In the 1800's, this native fish was so plentiful in the tributaries of the Rangeley Lakes that people pitch-forked them from the water and carried them off in cartloads for fertilizer. By 1900, they had seemingly disappeared from the state. Then, in 1948, a specimen was identified from a remote northern lake; an extensive search of more than 1,000 lakes and ponds has turned up populations of this beautiful trout in eight bodies of water in Maine. Today, they are highly protected.

The puffins, or "sea parrots," small, auk-like birds with colorful bills, constitute another rare species trying to make a comeback. In Penobscot Bay, some 125 nesting pairs are now established on various islands. At the turn of this century, they were almost totally depleted by hunters who sold their feathers to the millinery industry in New York, destroyed their eggs and used their carcasses for fish bait.

The razor bill auk also has begun to nest here again, but is even rarer — only 25 breeding pairs.

More prolific in Maine is still a third member of the auk family — the guillemot. It is estimated that there are now 3,000 breeding pairs nesting on 115 islands off the Maine coast.

Protection has increased the numbers of some sea birds dramatically, possibly even too much so. It is hard to believe that the ubiquitous herring gull (plain "sea gull" to most people) was once almost extinct in Maine at the end of the 19th century. Today there are more than 25,000 breeding pairs in Maine alone. Black-backed gulls are on the increase, too — over 10,000 breeding pairs. Cormorants are said to account for 16,000 pairs. Only the terns seem to be diminishing, possibly as a result of the explosion of the gull population.

Eider ducks represent another species that has staged a dramatic turnaround. They are now as numerous as the herring gulls — 25,000 breeding pairs. The comeback of the great blue heron and the snowy egret is apparent to any birdwatcher. The latter species are essentially more southern types increasing in their northern range. The same may also be true of the cardinal, now known to winter in southern and central Maine.

The news is good from the water as well. The Atlantic salmon, once driven from almost every Maine river by pollution and dams, is back. The old Maine custom of sending the first salmon caught in the Bangor Pool to the President of the United States has been reinstituted. Striped bass and bluefish, usually more southern fish, have been coming to Maine in growing numbers, providing exciting sport for Maine's salt water anglers.

At least one species new to Maine has not been greeted with enthusiasm. This is the coyote or, as this species of doglike predator is also called, "the brush wolf." The eastern coyote has spread to all parts of the state, prompting many sportsmen to call for measures to control the animal, including the use of bounties. The coyote is blamed for losses in the deer herd and for attacks on domestic animals. It is said to mate with domestic dogs and produce a "coy dog." The Department of Inland Fisheries and Wildlife has taken measures for intensive trapping of the coyote in areas where they are bothersome, but these measures have been criticized as inadequate by some sportsmen. Currently, about 600 coyotes are trapped in Maine each year.

The question of bounties for controlling nuisance animals has long been a controversial one in Maine. At the present time, there are no bounties on wildlife in the state. Bounties on bear, bobcat and porcupine have all been removed in recent years. The former two animals, in fact, are protected as valuable game species.

The increase in the moose herd in Maine recently led to another controversy. Groups opposed to the hunting of moose, mainly on the grounds that shooting these large, seemingly bovine animals does not constitute a sport, initiated a referendum by collecting enough signatures to place the question on a statewide ballot. Since 1980, the Legislature has authorized a limited moose hunt on the grounds that the herd, estimated at more than 20,000, had grown to the point where it could be prudently harvested. Moose hunting had previously been stopped in the state in 1935. On November 8, 1983, the voters by an almost 2-1 margin declined to repeal the moose hunt.

Maine people have strong feelings about their wildlife. Hunting and fishing are big business in Maine. But the attitudes of the past — that harvesting of fish and game can be unlimited — no longer dominate. Maine has more than 60 game sanctuaries and wildlife management areas. It has complex laws for the regulation of these activities and a force of nearly 135 wardens and deputy wardens to enforce them. The thrilling sight of clouds of passenger pigeons darkening the sky that John Josselyn saw in the 1600's will never be repeated. But at Merrymeeting Bay, 20th century Mainers and visitors to Maine can see the thousands of wild fowl that cross the state's path on the Atlantic Flyway. Whitetailed deer are probably far more abundant in Maine today (the grousing of contemporary hunters notwithstanding) than they were before the virgin forests were opened. Out of a herd estimated to be approximately 225,000, 28,000 to 31,000 on an average are shot each year. Some species are gone, never to be seen again. Other species, some new, some old, thrive as the attitudes of people toward the environment have changed. Maine people and the leaders of Maine people have been pioneers in the development of a new relationship with nature and wildlife. It is a deeply embedded item in the Maine tradition.

Head of a white-tailed deer, Maine's most popular game species.

Aerial view of a fishway.

The passenger pigeon. Millions of this now extinct bird once darkened the skies in Maine, as they did elsewhere in the nation.

The great auk. Slaughtered by the thousands along the Maine coast, this goose-sized bird became extinct in 1844.

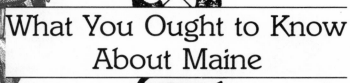

What You Ought to Know About Maine

L.L. BEAN

L. Bean! It is one of the country's most unusual — and most prestigious — retail outlets, and attests to Maine's interest in the outdoors. Known throughout the world for its catalogue, it also — in keeping with the image of the industrious Mainer — stays open 365 days a year, 24 hours a day.

It all began with a hunting trip. Leon Leonwood Bean, a young Maine man from the upcountry town of Bethel in northern Oxford County, then managing his brother's shoe store in Freeport, came back from the woods with sore, wet feet. Determined to improve his footwear, he went to a Freeport cobbler and had him cut bottoms from a pair of rubber boots and sew them to the uppers of a pair of leather boots. Thus was born the famous "Bean boots." At first, Bean only wore them himself and then had some made for friends who admired them. The reaction to his casual invention was so positive that he finally decided to borrow $400 and have 100 pairs made.

From this little acorn, an oak of a business grew. Bean marketed his 100 pairs of boots through the mail to holders of Maine hunting licenses and when many were returned in response to his unconditional guarantee, he had them reinforced and strengthened and would not consider the sale complete until assured of the customer's satisfaction.

In 1914, he opened a full-fledged business in a store across the street from the present L.L. Bean location. In 1917, he added hunting apparel and then fishing tackle and camping gear. By 1937, the store was grossing half-a-million dollars a year. It grew to three million dollars in 1966 and then leaped spectacularly to $56 million by 1978. Many famous people

The famous "Bean Boot" that launched L.L. Bean as a unique Maine retailer.

Leon Leonwood Bean, the original "L.L. Bean," shown modelling a wool coat for his first catalogue. A hunting trip inspired his unique Maine business.

The interior of the early L.L. Bean store. Long-time employee Howard Wilson is waiting on Mr. and Mrs. William Rand of Cundys Harbor.

have shopped there, including Babe Ruth, Jack Dempsey, Walter Cronkite and the explorer Admiral Donald MacMillan. When former Vice President Walter Mondale visited the state on one occasion, he announced that L.L. Bean's would be his first stop.

Letters have reached the store, addressed simply to "Bean, Maine."

L.L. Bean died in 1967. At the time, 50,000 people sent letters of condolence to his family, expressing sorrow for the passing of this extraordinary Maine man. Although orphaned at the age of 13 and with no more than an eighth-grade education, he had built a commercial empire out of the Maine values of hard work and offering full satisfaction for the money.

What You Ought to Know About Maine

THE UNORGANIZED TERRITORIES

Government in Maine has a few unique twists and turns that do not occur in any other state. One is the continued use of the "plantation" form of local government, an archaic system borrowed from Massachusetts and abandoned elsewhere, but still existing in 46 Maine communities. The other is the "unorganized territories" — actually more than half the land area of the state — which are mostly in private hands and mostly uninhabited while resting under the jurisdiction of the state government.

In the Western states large tracts of uninhabited land are under federal control. These are *public* lands. The situation of Maine's unorganized territories, in area more than 10 million acres, is basically unparalleled in the United States.

Before examining this curious happenstance, it is useful to have a brief picture of how Maine governs itself. As in all states, there are three branches essential for checks and balances — the Executive, the Legislative and the Judiciary.

The head of the Executive branch is, of course, the governor, elected by the people (in Maine the only official in the Executive to be popularly elected). The term is now four years — once, it was one year, then two years, and finally in 1957, the present length. Until 1975, the governor also had an Executive Council, not popularly elected, but chosen by the majority party in the Legislature, that could check and obstruct many gubernatorial actions. Since 1970, the governor has also been able to name co-terminous department heads.

The Legislature, composed of the House of Representatives of 151 members and the Senate now consisting of 33 members but soon to be increased to 35, passes the laws that the governor executes and the Judiciary — at least on the Supreme

Court level — determines to be or not to be in accordance with the state constitution. Judges are named by the governor and confirmed by the State Senate. Maine also has four constitutional officers chosen by the Legislature (usually by the majority party) — the attorney general, the secretary of state, the state treasurer and the state auditor. There is no lieutenant governor in Maine. If the governor dies or is incapacitated, the succession falls to the president of the Senate.

Cities in Maine (there are currently 22 of them) must be chartered by the State Legislature. Towns (there are 430) must be incorporated, which requires a legislative act but does not require a charter, which is like their own constitution. A town can simply operate under *state* statutes if it does not wish to draw up its own rules.

A "plantation" is a type of government that is something less than a town. It is not incorporated by the Legislature like a town but by the county commissioners of the county in which it is located. Nor does it have any rights under Home Rule as a town does. Home Rule allows a town to make many decisions without having to go to the Legislature. Most plantations are quite small, under 100 people, and the 46 existing today contain less than 7,000 people. For the most part, though, they do operate like mini-towns, with an annual meeting and assessors (not selectmen) elected to run the local government. (The term "assessor" has also been used for the officials who ran "village corporations" in Maine, a sort of government within a government that once frequently existed in the state but now is almost totally extinct.)

A word about counties in Maine. The county governments are said to be "creatures of the Legislature." Although the county commissioners are elected by the people, it is the Legislature that determines each county's budget. County functions are rather limited in Maine as they are throughout New England where the town unit has historically been more important. In many parts of the country, counties are very powerful, running the schools, the parks, the hospitals, etc.

So much for the organized half of the state. To understand how a vast area of wilderness without towns or even names of towns could be left in the northeast corner of the United

States, it is necessary to go back to the days just after the Revolution when Maine was still a "district" within the Commonwealth of Massachusetts.

Of all the thirteen colonies, Massachusetts had suffered the most onerous financial burdens of the War. Peace found the Bay State almost destitute. The greatest liquid asset that remained was the public lands owned by the government, most of which were located in Maine. Massachusetts made plans to sell them.

In 1783 a land office was established. But the sales went slowly. Next a lottery was tried but only 437 tickets out of 2,720 were sold. Land was then given away, or rather granted to institutions like schools and colleges or to towns that wanted to build roads, bridges, etc. — land that they could sell to use the proceeds for their own purposes. Veterans and the widows of veterans of the Revolution were rewarded with lands in Maine. Then, in 1793, the famous Bingham purchases were made by Robert Bingham of Philadelphia. At 12 and one-half cents an acre, he bought one million acres on the Kennebec and 1,107,396 million acres between the Penobscot and the St. Croix.

Until Maine's statehood in 1820, Massachusetts disposed of more than six million acres, adding to the almost four million that had earlier been granted by the King and the Plymouth Company in England.

When Maine separated from Massachusetts, however, it did not gain complete control of the remaining public land of almost 10 million acres. By the terms of the Articles of Separation, half of that land belonged to Massachusetts. An agreement for Maine to buy Massachusetts's share at four and one-half cents an acre was turned down by both legislatures in 1821. Ironically, when in 1852 Maine finally did buy out what was left to Massachusetts after it had disposed of three million acres, the price was 30 and one-half cents an acre.

By 1878, after almost five million acres had been sold or granted for railroad projects by Maine, the land agent could report that "all the public lands of the state having been disposed of, no further favors are now within the power of the state to grant for homesteads to settlers."

In many of these areas today, road signs will identify not the name of the town but a mysterious set of letters, and numbers, such as T3 R4, or *Township 3 Range 4*. But that isn't all. It might be T3 R4 W.E.L.S., or T3 R4 N.B.K.P., or T3 R4 B.K.P.W.K.R. These three are all different townships (a "township," not to be confused with a town, is an area of six square miles or 23,000 acres), but each has the same beginning designation — T3 R4 — although located in three different parts of the state. W.E.L.S. stands for "West of East Line of State." N.B.K.P. stands for "North of Bingham Kennebec Purchase." And B.K.P.W.K.R. stands for "Bingham Kennebec Purchase, West of Kennebec River." It gets even more complicated, too.

Every township of 23,000 acres was laid out as if someday it would develop into an inhabited town. Several lots within each one, amounting to 1,000 acres, were reserved for the support of a future school teacher and a future minister of the gospel. These are the so-called "Public Reserved Lots" that have been the source of great controversy over the years. Originally, when the state sold the wildlands, it only sold the grass and timber rights on these reserved lots. Recently the State Supreme Judicial Court declared that these grass and timber rights were not sold forever and that the lots now belong to the state. At issue are more than 400,000 acres of land, much of which has been recovered by the state government in the past few years.

Lumbering began in Maine with the first settlers. An economic mainstay of the early colonists was the production of shingles and of staves for barrels and hogsheads. The Crown government in England soon recognized the value of Maine pines for Royal Navy masts. Slowly, as the most commercially valuable trees were cut, the industry moved north. From 1820 to 1880, lumbering for saw logs was the state's most important economic activity. By 1840, Bangor was the logging capital of the entire country. In 1880, a new development began — the pulp and paper industry. It is now the dominant force in the Maine economy.

The existence of large-scale logging in the northern half of Maine, whether for sawlogs or for pulpwood, tended to discourage settlement, which ordinarily would have led to agricultural development as it did in the potato fields of Aroostook County. Furthermore, the large landowners, as they consolidated their holdings and devoted them to wood use, followed a deliberate policy of discouraging the introduction of people to their area. Thus the greater part of northern Maine has remained unpopulated and consequently "unorganized." While this situation has conferred undoubted benefits upon the state and the private landowners, it also has created some problems.

The question of how to govern this vast wilderness (there are *some* people who live in it) was always a problem. One of Maine's motivations in selling off the land was that the state could not protect it. Timber thieves often roamed the woods at will, taking what trees they wanted with no one to stop them. The state through its land agent reasoned that a private owner would be willing and able to put a stop to these depredations.

Yet private responsibility was not all-inclusive enough to deal with certain other basic problems — the most critical of which was fire.

Until 1891, the State land agent was the government official most responsible for the wildlands. In 1891 the Legislature transformed him into the forest commissioner. In the unorganized territories, the county commissioners were directed to appoint fire wardens.

This embryo of today's Forest Service took a number of years to develop. An important change was made in 1903 when money to fight forest fires was appropriated for the first time. Not coincidentally, 1903 was a year in which 200,232 acres in the unorganized territories were burned (a doleful record not exceeded until 1947). In 1909 the precedent-setting Maine Forestry District was created, a model for the rest of the country in, as one landowner put it, "the preventative maintenance and control of forest lands against fire."

Within the Maine Forestry District, an area of about 10 million acres, a small tax was levied and the proceeds used to fund the organization necessary to combat fires in the area. A measure of its effectiveness is that a recent 400-acre fire in the Chesuncook area was considered one of the largest in years; contrast this with the 200,232 acres burnt in 1903 or even the 98,691 acres lost in 1908, one year before the M.F.D. was created. Although changed in various ways through the years, the district system remained in effect until the 111th Legislature in 1983 eliminated it in favor of a statewide forest fire protection land tax. Meanwhile, the Maine Forest Service continues to be the fire department for the unorganized territories, but will no longer perform that function for plantations.

A typical fire tower — one of the 27 remaining in Maine.

The Maine Department of Education and Cultural Affairs pays the tuition of most of the pupils within the area to schools outside of it. But in addition, the department runs five elementary schools, itself. The mechanism through which it does this is a bureau called E.U.T. (Education in the Unorganized Territories). It used to be called S.C.U.T. (Schooling of Children in the Unorganized Territories) but the name was changed to reflect the fact that it also handles adult education. This state agency hires and fires teachers and pays all of the costs of the programs it runs, a departure from the rest of the state where control of the schools and at least half the funding is a local affair.

Finally, there is the matter of land planning and zoning of the unorganized territories, also a function usually reserved

A forest fire burning in Maine.

for local communities. In 1969, the Legislature created the Land Use Regulation Commission to accomplish this purpose. This agency, which like the Forest Service is now located within the Department of Conservation, acts as the zoning board for this entire 10 million acre parcel of land, providing both long term and short term planning plus enforcement of its rules through a permit system. Its activities have not been without controversy in its interaction with private landowners, accustomed to doing what they wished on their own land.

The unorganized territories are not simply a howling wilderness full of moose and bear. Visitors to them will often find as much traffic on their woods roads as on thoroughfares in the organized portions of the state — logging trucks by the score or a steady stream of Maine fishermen, hunters and campers entering the area for recreational reasons. The North Maine Woods is an umbrella organization of landowners formed to manage some two million acres of wildlands that the public is allowed to use — for a fee — for recreation. In the unorganized territories, one will find homes, schools, lumber camps, summer homes on lease lots, airports, various commercial operations and, in the future possibly, mining activity. It is a unique resource that a unique history has bequeathed to the State of Maine. It is something, obviously, that people ought to know about Maine.

ROUND

Toss-Up Questions

1 In 1905, the first of its kind in the United States was established on Maine's Squaw Mountain. What was it?

2 What is Maine's longest county from one end to another? It is also Maine's second largest county in total land area.

3 Acadia National Park was originally known as the "Sieur de Monts National Monument," in honor of the French nobleman who originally sent out parties of colonists to the area.

In 1919, when it became the first national park east of the Mississippi, it was not named Acadia.

What was its first name, which it kept for ten years until it did officially become Acadia National Park?

4 In Kennebunk, there stands a stately elm tree that was supposedly planted on the day of the battles of Lexington and Concord. For what Revolutionary War hero is this tree named?

5 Which of the following types of tree is *not* a hardwood tree?
  Beech?
  Maple?
  Yellow birch?
  Hemlock?

6 Portland is Maine's busiest seaport. What town, known as the "Home of Famous Sea Captains," is Maine's second busiest seaport?

Answers to Toss-Up Questions

1 The first forest fire lookout tower.

At present, 27 lookout towers are still being operated by the Maine Forest Service. A controversial plan to close a number of them was resisted by the 111th Maine Legislature. At one time, there were more than 100 towers in Maine, but the use of air patrols, particularly in the uninhabited northern areas has cut down on the need for their use. Strong arguments are continually made by fire fighting groups that towers are essential for communication in the more populated areas of the state.

2 Somerset County.

It extends from the Canadian border to Fairfield, a distance of 150 miles. Its land area is 3,903.9 square miles, a good deal behind Aroostook, which has 6,450.7 square miles, and slightly ahead of Piscataquis with its 3,809.5 square miles. The forested portion of Somerset County is 90 percent and it borders Moosehead Lake and the Allagash Wilderness Waterway. The county seat, Skowhegan, is the site of one of Maine's largest agricultural fairs.

3 Lafayette National Park.

4 The Marquis de Lafayette.

Lafayette made a memorable trip to Maine in 1825, where he was greeted as a long-time friend and genuine national hero. In Kennebunk, he stood under this particular elm during a reception there in his honor. At Portland, which was then the state capital, the welcoming speech was given by Stephen Longfellow, father of the future poet. On hand, too, was Albion Parris, the governor of Maine, and the Marquis's son, George Washington Lafayette.

In the toasts that were given that day, the young Lafayette drank to "Yankee Doodle, the oldest and gayest death-song to despotism."

And the Marquis, after having declared, "I found in George Washington a father and Henry Knox a brother," made the following toast:

"To the state of Maine who, yet an infant and not weaned from its mother, gallantly helped in crushing European aristocracy and despotism; and to the town of Portland, which rose from the ashes of patriotic Falmouth to become the flourishing metropolis of a flourishing State . . ."

5 Hemlock.

Hemlock is an evergreen and all evergreens are softwoods.

6 Searsport.

During the age of sail, Searsport was a noted shipbuilding center, as well as the port of call for numerous foreign trading vessels. A century ago, the town produced one-tenth of all deep water shipmasters in the American Merchant Marine. It is the site of the Penobscot Marine Museum, comprised of six separate buildings connected with those days.

Toss-Up Questions

Note: Lazy Lester was a character invented by one of the producers of "So You Think You Know Maine" as a vehicle for posing certain types of questions. He had a sister named Mean Margaret, who also entered the quiz game. This page of Toss-Up Questions is devoted to that deliberately cutesy Down East pair.

7 Lazy Lester's mother told him to get a couple of "golden eyes." Poor Lester was confused because he didn't know what he was looking for. Please help him.

8 Mean Margaret told her brother Lazy Lester that silviculture was very important in Maine. Lazy Lester said that was passing strange to him because he didn't know they had any silver in Maine. Was Lester right?

9 Mean Margaret told Lazy Lester about a great new restaurant in town called the "Legal Eagle" and said that it served the best venison stew. When Lester went there, he found he couldn't get any of the stew. How come?

10 Lazy Lester heard that Maine's "Old Sow" was really something to see. Where would he have to go to view it?
  a. A pig farm?   b. The ocean?   c. A Miss Piggy Special?

11 Mean Margaret fixed up a potion made with pulverized sugar wet down with an equal amount of wine vinegar and gave it to Lazy Lester to cure her brother of what?

12 Lazy Lester wanted to visit the Indian tribes in Maine. Which one among the following would he not have found?
  a. Penobscots?   b. Malecites?   c. Mohawks?
  d. Passamaquoddies?

13 Lazy Lester's mother is often heard to say, "I wish you were the *driver* your father is!" She isn't talking about his ability to operate an automobile. What does she wish Lester was?

14 If Lazy Lester could drive an automobile, would he be able to handle a "lobster car?"

7 Golden eyes are ducks.

These small diving ducks with glittery little yellow eyes are primarily sea ducks. Of course, you know the recipe Lazy Lester's mother would use for cooking up sea ducks. She'd boil some water, put in the ducks and a big stone, cook for a long time, then throw away the ducks and eat the stone. (That's a joking way of saying that sea ducks are pretty tough to chew and don't taste any too elegant, either.)

8 No way.

Silviculture refers to the growing of trees.

9 It's against the law to sell venison in Maine.

If they had had it on the menu, the place would have been the "Illegal Eagle."

10 The ocean.

The "Old Sow" is in Passamaquoddy Bay. It is one of the world's biggest whirlpools.

11 Hiccups.

Mean Margaret wasn't being mean, just old-fashioned. This was a tried if not necessarily true Maine home remedy in the past.

12 Mohawks

The Mohawks, from New York State, were members of the Iroquois Confederation. Their language was different from the Algonquian tongues spoken by the Maine tribes and there was deadly enmity between them. Often, the Mohawks raided Maine.

13 A hard worker.

14 Not likely.

A "lobster car" is a floating raft contraption in which lobsters are stored at sea.

Note: Viewers often send in suggestions for questions to "So You Think You Know Maine." The following is a sampling of some of the questions that have been proposed.

15 Maine's first town, incorporated on November 20, 1652, was Kittery. Where does the name Kittery come from?

a. A town in County Mayo, Ireland?   b. A Pequawket Indian name?   c. An estate in Devonshire, England?

16 When Maine became a state in 1820, how many congressional districts did it have?

17 General Henry Knox, Washington's secretary of war, and the resident of Thomaston for whom Knox County is named, founded the Society of the Cincinnati. What was this organization?

a. A baseball team?   b. A veterans' organization?   c. A group studying Latin?

18 When Portland was burned in the Great Fire of 1876, some of its burned out residents were given free tracts of land in another township up country. Name that community.

19 King Philip's War, the first conflict with the Indians in Maine, originally broke out in Massachusetts. Why did the fighting spread north?

a. The Massachusetts Indians convinced their Maine brethren to join in the fray?

b. French agents incited the Maine Indians to attack?

c. Some drunken English sailors drowned the baby son of an Indian chief in the Saco River?

20 Several towns in Maine have been named after governors of Massachusetts. Thomas Pownal was one and William Shirley another. Pownal is in Cumberland County. Where is Shirley?

15 An estate in Devonshire, England.

Kittery, which beat York out by two days to become the first incorporated town in Maine, was named for a manor house on an island in the Dart River. Many of Kittery's early settlers came from Devonshire — one of the counties in England's "West Country." These included the father and maternal grandparents of Sir William Pepperell, Kittery's most famous native son.

16 Seven.

1st. District: York County.
2nd. District: Cumberland County.
3rd. District: Lincoln County.
4th. District: Kennebec County.
5th. District: Oxford County
6th. District: Hancock and Washington Counties.
7th. District: Somerset and Penobscot Counties.

17 A veterans' organization.

This association formed of Washington's ex-officers was named for Cincinnatus, the Roman general who had also been a farmer and was noted for having left his plow to go to war and then returning to his fields as soon as possible. In other words, a symbol of the citizen soldier. Those foreign officers from France, Germany, Poland, etc. who had fought with the Americans were also members of the society.

18 New Portland, in Somerset County, current population: 646.

19 The outrageous act of the drunken English sailors.

The sailors decided to test a theory that all Indian babies knew instinctively how to swim. When a canoe carrying the wife of Chief Squanto and her infant son passed by, they deliberately overturned it. The baby sank and although the frantic mother finally fished him out of the water, he died soon afterward. The Indians exacted a fearsome revenge in their subsequent attacks throughout Maine.

20 Piscataquis County.

It has a population of 241 and is close to the border of Somerset County.

21 The controversial Fernald Law, a Maine statute since repealed, enforced a regulation on one of the following types of utilities:
   Telephones?
   Electric power?
   Sewer districts?

22 President William Howard Taft visited Portland in 1912. Who was the next president to visit the Forest City?

23 William Pitt Fessenden was a Maine politician who helped found the Republican Party in the state. He was a U.S. senator and Lincoln's Secretary of the Treasury and a leader of the "Radical Republicans" whose program was to punish the South after the Civil War. In 1868, Fessenden did something in Washington, D.C. that made him very unpopular at home. What was it?

24 The National Geographic Society has placed a granite boulder in Maine marking the point that lies midway between the North Pole and the equator. It is located on Route 1 just north of what town?

25 A colony of tiny Syrians is living in a segregated housing development on Mount Desert Island. They are bright-eyed and curious, but given to occasional fits of restlessness and bad temper. The management, however, has found that soft music will soothe their nerves. Who are these mysterious strangers?

21 Electric power.

The Fernald Law forbade the exporting of power generated within Maine to any other state. The reasoning behind it was that if industry wanted Maine's electric power, they should have to locate in Maine in order to use it. The Fernald Law was repealed in 1955.

22 President Lyndon B. Johnson in 1964.

23 Fessenden voted against the impeachment of President Andrew Johnson.

President Andrew Johnson was extremely unpopular in Maine if for no other reason than that he had replaced Maine's own Hannibal Hamlin, Lincoln's first vice president, who had been pushed aside to make room for Johnson on the G.O.P. ticket in 1864. As a southerner, Johnson tried to block the harsh policies of the Radical Republicans. Their impeachment move against him failed by one vote. Fessenden's unexpected vote not to impeach was considered an act of treachery. A little more than a year later, severely depressed by the hostility he encountered from colleagues and constituents, Fessenden died. Not one but three Portland streets are named after him: William Street, Pitt Street and Fessenden Street.

24 Perry, in Washington County.

25 Hamsters of Syrian ancestry at the famed Jackson Laboratory.

Bar Harbor's Jackson Laboratory is noted world-wide for its cancer research and particularly for the experimental rodents that it breeds to be used in medical research. "Jackson mice" are sent all over the world for genetic studies.

A QUICKY

In the town of Albion, a certain elm-shaded street bears a peculiar history. On the south side are the "Water Elms" and on the north side, the "Rum Elms." They were planted in a contest between the village temperance group and anti-Prohibitionists in 1845. Whose elms grew best, they agreed, would be considered the one most favored by the Providence. The "Rum Elms" today give broader shade than the "Water Elms."

26 What traditional Maine dish would you prepare with the following ingredients?

    1 quart of milk, scalded.
    ¼ cup corn meal
    1 cup molasses
    1 cup brown sugar
    2 cups seeded raisins
    ½ cup butter
    2 teaspoons vanilla
    1 teaspoon salt
    1 teaspoon cinnamon
    4 eggs
    2 cans of evaporated milk (13 ounce cans)

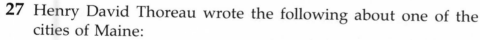

27 Henry David Thoreau wrote the following about one of the cities of Maine:

"There it stands like a star on the edge of night, still hewing at the forest of which it is built, already overflowing with the luxuries and refinements of Europe and sending its vessels to Spain, to England and to the West Indies for its groceries."

What city was he describing?

28 Who wrote:

"I am not a politician and my other habits are also good."

Answers to Toss-Up Questions

26 Baked Indian pudding.

The rest of the recipe goes as follows: Sprinkle corn meal into the scalded milk and whip. Place in double boiler and cook for 10 minutes, stirring to keep smooth. Mix together in baking pan 8 by 14 inches the other ingredients and pour hot corn meal over them and mix well. Cook in slow oven, 250 degrees for four hours and stir thoroughly every 15 to 20 minutes. Serve hot with vanilla ice cream.

27 Bangor.

Thoreau was describing Bangor during the heyday of the lumbering industry. There are nine other cities in the United States with the name of Bangor — in Pennsylvania, Michigan, Wisconsin, Washington, New York, Alabama, California, Kentucky and Iowa, and one formerly in South Dakota that has disappeared. There are two Bangors in Canada, one in Saskatchewan and another on Prince Edward Island, one in Northern Ireland, three in Wales, one in South Africa and one in France.

28 Artemus Ward.

The Oxford County-born humorist also wrote:

"At a special Congressional election in my district the other day I deliberately voted for Henry Clay. I admit that Henry is dead, but in as much as we don't have a live statesman in our National Congress, let us by all means have a first-class corpse."

A QUICKY

In the Rockland area, a famous cave is supposedly located on the shore of Hardwood Island, one that extends 80 feet underground. Before the Civil War, the ship "Rover" was wrecked in the vicinity and a lone survivor lived in the cave, venturing out at night to local farms to snatch livestock and crops for food. Then, the plundering abruptly stopped. Some years later, a letter came from France, addressed to the people of the area. It was signed "Captain X.Y.Z." and contained a 100 franc note along with an apology for the victuals he'd stolen and directions on how to reach the cave where he'd hidden. All that was found in the cave was a board with the name "Rover" on it.

Toss-Up Questions

29 John Josselyn, in 1672, wrote the following description of a common Maine animal that he said lived in hollow trees and fed on Indian corn:

"They will be exceedingly fat in Autumn, their flesh is somewhat dark but good food when roasted. Their fat is excellent for bruises and aches. Their skins are a good deep fur, but yet as the wild cats, somewhat coarse."

What animal is he describing?

30 What fish is being described by this 17th century Maine visitor?

". . . in April there is a fish that comes up small brooks to spawn and when the water is not knee deep, they will press up through your hands, yea, though you beat them with cudgels and in such abundance as is incredible."

31 The famous writer Willa Cather once stated:

"If I were asked to name three American books that have the possibility of long life, I would say *Huckleberry Finn*, *The Scarlet Letter*, and *The Country of the Pointed Firs*.

What Maine writer wrote *The Country of Pointed Firs*?

32 What did this Maine newspaper headline on July 24, 1981 mean?

"HAND-CRANKED YIELDS TO TOUCH TONE"

29 The raccoon.

30 The alewife.

Alewives are anadromous fish, meaning they spend most of their lives in the sea, but ascend freshwater streams to spawn. Other names for them are spring herring, branch herring, big-eyed herring, ellwife, ellwhop, goggle-eye, sawbelly, greyback and Kennebec turkey.

John Josselyn wrote of the species:

"The Alewife is like a Herrin', but has a bigger belly; therefore called an alewife."

31 Sarah Orne Jewett.

Sarah Orne Jewett, probably the finest writer Maine has ever produced, grew up and lived all of her life in South Berwick. Her father was a country doctor and she often accompanied him on his house calls. Her books and stories are sensitive depictions of everyday Maine life. As fellow Maine author Robert P. Tristram Coffin said, "She was the first writer of us all to get down on paper the good bedrock of Maine character and color." Rudyard Kipling said to her of her work, "It's immense . . . it is the very life . . . I don't believe even you know how good that work is." In 1901, she was the first woman to receive an honorary doctorate from then all-male Bowdoin College.

32 The sale of the Bryant Pond Telephone Company.

The Bryant Pond Telephone Company had the last hand-cranked magneto telephones in the United States. They at last yielded to so-called "progress" when the firm was sold to the Oxford County Telephone and Telegraph Company.

Toss-Up Questions

33 On which Kennebec River island will you find the only campground that is operated by the Maine Department of Inland Fisheries and Wildlife?

34 The world's most powerful radio station is located in a Washington County town. The station, owned and operated by the U.S. Navy, covers the North Atlantic, Arctic and Mediterranean areas. What is the name of the town that houses this station?

35 Maine has a national park, many state parks and even a county park. But does it have an international park?

36 Name the first governor of Maine after the Civil War. He was a returning war hero who had been a college professor and an ordained minister. He was one of Maine's most popular governors.

37 In 1733, the first limestone quarry in Maine was opened in which of the following locations.
Rockport? Thomaston? Rockland?

38 Edmund S. Muskie has had a distinguished career in Maine public life. He has been a legislator, a governor, a U.S. senator and America's Secretary of State. He is the son of Polish immigrant parents. In which Maine community was he born?
Waterville? Kennebunk? Rumford?

33 Swan Island.

This island is not to be confused with Swan's Island, which is in Hancock County, south of Bar Harbor. Swan Island has also been called "Swango" or "Island of the Eagles," the name given to it by the Kennebec Indians.

34 Cutler.

35 Yes, Maine does have an international park.

It is Campobello-Roosevelt International Memorial Park located on Campobello Island. Although Campobello is Canadian soil, the park has a joint American-Canadian commission that administers it and both countries dedicated this memorial, the site of Franklin Delano Roosevelt's summer home, in 1964. The national park in Maine, of course, is Acadia National park and the county park is Mattawamkeag Wilderness Park in Penobscot County, a 1,018 acre wilderness area off Route 2 on the Mattawamkeag and Penobscot Rivers. There are 29 state parks, including the Allagash Wilderness Waterway and Baxter State Park.

36 Joshua L. Chamberlain.

Joshua Lawrence Chamberlain was born in Brewer. A large part of his life was spent in Brunswick, where he went to school, taught at Bowdoin and later became the college's president. As commander of the 20th Maine regiment, General Chamberlain achieved lasting fame for his defense of the Little Round Top height of land against the attacking Texas and Alabama troops of General James Longstreet. After four years as governor of Maine, a post he acquired in 1867, Chamberlain returned to Bowdoin and presided as its chief officer for the next twelve years.

It was Chamberlain whom General Ulysses S. Grant chose to receive the Confederate surrender at Appomatox. He described the scene in these rather eloquent words:

"On our part, not a sound of trumpet more, nor roll of drum; not a cheer, nor word nor whisper of vain-glorying . . . but an awed stillness rather, and breath-holding, as if it were the passing of the dead. They tenderly folded their flags, battleworn and torn, and laid them down, and then only the Flag of the Union greeted the sky."

37 Thomaston.

The state prison is located on the site of the first quarry.

38 Rumford.

Edmund Sixtus Muskie moved to Waterville as a young lawyer and was elected to represent it in the Maine House. Today, he makes his home in Kennebunk.

Toss-Up Questions

39 The following names of towns in Maine all have something in common:
Pepperrellborough.
Cushnoc.
Gorgeana.
What is it?

40 What is special about Peter Dana Point and Pleasant Point, both of which are located in Washington County?

41 Lincoln, Maine, Lincolnville, Maine and Lincoln County, Maine also all have something in common. What is it?

42 Governor James Bowdoin of Massachusetts (1785–86) gave his name to Bowdoin College. His family owned extensive lands in Maine. The Bowdoins donated the land and money necessary to establish the college, which opened in 1802 with eight students. True or false? James Bowdoin was of French descent.

43 The largest city in Maine is Portland (population 61,572), the smallest city is Eastport (population 1,982), the smallest town is Bowerbank (population 27). What is the largest town?

44 Maine's State bird is the black-capped chickadee. The State mineral is tourmaline. The State flower is the white pine cone and tassel. The State animal is the moose and the State fish is the landlocked salmon. Which of the following is the State insect?
The spruce budworm? The firefly? The honeybee?

39 They are the former names of present-day communities.

Pepperrellborough is Saco. It was named for Sir William Pepperrell, the hero of Louisbourg, who also owned most of the land on which the town of Saco now stands. It was said he could ride from his house at Kittery Point to Scarborough and never get off his own land.

Cushnoc is Augusta.

Gorgeanna is York. It was named after Sir Ferdinando Gorges, who envisioned the town as an English city, the center of his "Palatinate" or private province of Maine. The name was changed to York in honor of Oliver Cromwell's capture of the English city of the same name.

40 They are both Indian reservations.

These are the two homes of the Passamaquoddy tribe. Peter Dana Point is near Princeton and involves two areas: the "Strip," a living area, and a 23,000 acre township of forested wilderness. Pleasant Point is close to Eastport and borders the sea. Since the Indian Land Claims settlement, the tribe has bought considerably more land.

41 None of them are named for Abraham Lincoln.

Lincoln, Maine is named for Enech Lincoln, Maine's sixth governor. Lincolnville, Maine is named for General Benjamin Lincoln, a prominent soldier in the American Revolution and an incorporator of the town. Lincoln County, Maine is named for Thomas Pownal, a colonial governor of Massachusetts whose home was Lincoln, England.

42 True.

The Bowdoins were Huguenots, French Protestants, who had been driven out of France at the time of the Revocation of the Edict of Nantes, 1685. Many came as refugees to New England and were soon Anglicized. The original family name of the Bowdoins was Beaudoin. Paul Revere was also of Huguenot descent. His original family name was Rivoire.

43 Sanford (population 18,020).

Despite its good-sized population, Sanford still maintains a town meeting-selection form of government, but it is a "representative" town meeting. In order to vote, one must be elected as a town meeting member, although anyone in town is eligible to speak and otherwise participate.

44 The honeybee.

The honeybee was chosen by the State Legislature to be the State insect as a result of a bill prepared by a fourth-grade class in Kennebunk studying government. The youngsters went through the entire legislative process and saw the bill that they had drafted and proposed win out over another bill, put in by fourth graders from the Mark Emery School, North Anson, that suggested the monarch butterfly as the State insect.

Category Questions

3

MAINE EVENTS

1 When was the first *state-approved* lottery conducted in Maine? 1819? 1900? 1823?

2 Although the Portland and Oxford Central Railroad was short-lived, one event in its brief history continues to amaze historians. What great feat was accomplished in a desperate attempt to run a train to Canton Village?

3 David Robinson, an ice dealer, supposedly invented this special delicacy for the enjoyment of the Marquis de Lafayette during Lafayette's visit to Portland in 1825. What was it?

4 True or False? The people in Madawaska look forward each year to the "Miss Dumpy" pageant.

5 In 1970, Armand A. Dufresne became the first Franco-American to be appointed chief justice of the Maine Supreme Judicial Court. Which governor appointed him?

6 When Samuel de Champlain cruised the Maine coast in 1605, he landed at what is now known as Richmond's Island. He found something growing so plentifully that he named the island "Isle of Bacchus." What was it that he found?

7 A TV movie based on one of Rudyard Kipling's famed adventure stories was filmed in Maine within the last three years. What is the name of the book and the film?

8 Identify the following.
"I am the largest in the world, measuring ten and a half feet across." "I can be seen in Pittsfield during the "Central Maine Egg Festival" held the last Saturday in July."

Answers to Category Questions

1 1823.

The State Legislature granted the Cumberland and Oxford Canal Corporation the right to conduct a lottery to raise $50,000. Prior to this, numerous local lotteries were held in order to raise money for projects such as bridges and public buildings. In 1973, the State Legislature created the Maine State Lottery whose purpose is to raise general fund money for the running of the State.

2 It ran tracks across the ice.

In the dead of winter, tracks were laid across frozen Canton Lake and the railroad ran a train to Canton Village. The nearly bankrupt railroad thus hoped to collect $30,000 authorized by the town of Canton if rail service to it was completed by a certain time. Of course, when spring came and the ice melted, the tracks disappeared.

3 Ice cream.

Robinson froze a mixture of custard and allegedly produced the first ice cream.

4 False.

It's the people of Kennebunkport who look forward to the "Miss Dumpy" pageant. The brainchild of artist Ed Mayo, the Kennebunkport Dump Pageant and the publicity that surrounds it is intended to bring home the message of environmental betterment through parody and caricature.

5 Kenneth M. Curtis.

Curtis was also the governor who appointed the first Maine Indian to head up the Bureau of Indian Affairs and the first student to be on the Board of Trustees of the University of Maine.

6 Grapes.

7 "Captains Courageous"

It was filmed in Camden and around the islands of Penobscot Bay. A famous feature film of this story of fishing off the Grant Banks was made in 1937, starring Spencer Tracy and Freddy Bartholomew.

8 The world's largest frying pan.

Category Questions 3

ENERGY

9 In 1974, a Liberian tanker, the "Argo Merchant," was responsible for an oil spill in which Maine port?

10 How does Portland rank in size among oil ports on the east coast of the United States?
 Smallest?
 Second largest?
 Tenth largest?

11 There are several large heaths and bogs in Maine that contain a minable substance known to be useful for fuel and horticulture. What is this substance?

12 Which of the following Maine trees has the highest number of BTU's when burned?
 White pine?
 White birch?
 Elm?
 Apple?

13 Because of the current energy crisis, a project is underway to harness what natural force in Passamaquoddy Bay to produce electricity?

14 In 1977, what percent of Maine's annual utility-generated electrical power came from hydropower?
 2%? 11%? 22%?

15 What are the dimensions, in feet, of a cord of wood?

16 What is the name of Maine's largest hydroelectric dam?

Answers to Category Questions

9 Portland.

10 Second largest.

Philadelphia, the site of a number of oil refineries, is the largest oil port on the east coast. The reason for Portland's position of second place as an oil port is the presence there of the Montreal pipeline. All oil going to the Canadian metropolis must pass through Portland. In 1971, Maine legislators, worried about the danger of oil spills, passed the "Oil Conveyance Law," the first measure of its kind in the country. It set up a "superfund" to be used to pay for the immediate clean-up of oil spills, the money coming from a per-barrel tax charged to the pipeline.

11 Peat.

Maine has huge quantities of peat in hundreds of bogs and heaths, like the "Great Heath" of Washington County. Recently, there has been some interest in the commercial use of this resource for fuel and there is already some limited mining of peat for the gardening market. The Wheelabrator-Frye Company of Hampton, New Hampshire has a proposal for developing the peat resources of the Sunk-Haze Bog in Penobscot County.

12 Apple.

13 The tides.

In some places in this area, there is a difference of at least 14 feet in tides. The current proposal is for a project in Nova Scotia, but previously, in the late 1920's and early 1930's, the "Quoddy" project of Dexter Cooper almost saw the light of day. However, after some initial work, it was halted due to political considerations and never re-started. There has been some interest by the Passamaquoddy Indians in a small project in Cobscook Bay, which would be the American site for any effort to build a dam, as the French have done in Brittany, to control the immense force of the tides in order to produce electricity.

14 22%.

There are 125 hydroelectric dams now operating in Maine.

15 Eight feet long, four feet wide, four feet high.

In all, 128 cubic feet.

16 Wyman Dam.

It was completed in 1931 and named for Walter Wyman, the founder of the Central Maine Power Company.

Category Questions

3

PLACES

17 Name the island off the coast of Knox County that was used as a fishing base by early explorers such as Captain George Waymouth and Captain John Smith.

18 Is Indian Island an island?

19 What do the following Maine counties have in common?
Androscoggin. Sagadahoc. Kennebec. Penobscot.
Piscataquis. Aroostook.

20 One of the three examples of authentic Victorian architecture in the United States is situated in Portland. It is included in the National Register of Historic Places and features a flying staircase and seven Carrara marble mantels and fireplaces that were hand carved in Italy. It was built for Ruggles Sylvester Morse who presented it to his bride. What is this landmark?

21 True or False? The mouth of the Kennebec River is located at Moosehead Lake?

22 This popular tourist attraction was once the site of a fertile farm that eventually disappeared under an ancient deposit of glacial sand. Where is this natural curiosity located?

23 Everyone knows that Mount Katahdin is in Baxter State Park. But in what park can these lesser known mountains be found? North Bubble Mountain, the Beehive, Sargent Mountain?

24 In early colonial days, Kennebunkport was known as:
Jimmybunkport? Billybunkport? Cape Porpoise?

Answers to Category Questions

17 Monhegan Island.

As one of the outermost islands off the coast of Maine, Monhegan attracted passing sailors as early as the 1500's when fishermen from Europe set up the fish-drying stages on its soil. In 1603, the ships "Speedwell" and "Discovered", sent out by Sir Humphrey Gilbert and his half brother Sir Walter Raleigh, stopped at Monhegan long enough to pick up a birchbark canoe left there by some Indians, which they brought back to England where it was a sensation. Waymouth, on his trip a few years later, reached the Maine coast and carried back something even more sensational — five live Indians who he kidnapped. Captain John Smith, although associated in most minds with Virginia, spend a good deal of time along the New England coast. The Isles of Shoals were said originally to have been named "Smith's Isles." His stay at Monhegan is today commemorated by a plaque on the island.

18 Yes.

It is part of Old Town and is connected to that city by a one-lane bridge across the Penobscot River. It is the home of about 1,200 Penobscot Indians. It was a portion of land that they retained after a treaty with Massachusetts, signed on October 11, 1786, whereby the tribe ceded most of its holdings for 300 blankets and 200 pounds of gunpowder and shot and flints.

19 They all have Indian names.

20 The Victoria Mansion.

21 False.

Moosehead Lake is the *source* of the Kennebec River. Merrymeeting Bay is the *mouth* of the Kennebec where it empties into the Atlantic Ocean.

22 Freeport.

It is the so-called "Desert of Maine." Shallow soil, located atop bottomless sand, contributed to this odd phenomenon that has for many years been a major tourist curiosity in Maine. It has been surmised that grazing sheep or fire killed the roots of the grass meadow originally here and allowed the desert to surface. Just as the Sahara spreads each year, so has the "Desert of Maine" grown, helped by wind-blown sand.

23 Acadia National Park.

24 Cape Porpoise.

A "Cape Porpoise" section exists in present-day Kennebunkport. Another name for this general York County region is "Arundel," after the Earl of Arundel who received a vast grant in the area. The present Arundel is a town of about 2,000 people.

Category Questions

3

DOWN EAST LINGO

25 When a hunter returns from a trip and tells you that he got a real "cruncher," what does he mean?

26 If someone delivers you a "jag" of wood, have you gotten your money's worth?

27 Lazy Lester's mother was often heard to say, "That boy is so gawmy." What did she mean by "gawmy?"

28 Explain what is meant when a farmer says he put "dressing" on his fields.

29 Should you be offended if someone calls your house a "gut bucket?"

30 Where would you be hurting if you were suffering from a bruised "prayer handle?"

31 When you are suffering from a hangover, what might look like "two burnt holes in a blanket?"

32 You have been described as a person who "goes with your head up and your tail over the dashboard." Are you considered: A bad driver?   A proud person?
A person who walks like a duck?

33 Lazy Lester's father told him to go and get some "crocus sacks." Poor Lester dug up all the crocusses in his mother's garden. But what did Lester's father really want?

34 Here are three different sizes of inlet: An "eel rut." A "gunk hole." A "guzzle hole." Which is the largest?

25 A "cruncher" is a real large deer.

26 Yes.
A "jag" of wood is a full load, so full, in fact, that one more stick would fall off.

27 Clumsy or awkward.

28 He is spreading cow or horse manure all over his fields in order to fertilize them.

29 Yes, indeed.
A "gut bucket" is a very untidy place.

30 Your knee is your "prayer handle."

31 Your eyes.

32 A proud person.

33 Burlap Bags.

34 A "guzzle hole."
A "guzzle hole" is a place along the coast where one would find a store that also sold gasoline.

1 The Blaine House was built in 1833, but it did not become the official residence of Maine's governors until Carl E. Milliken became the state's chief executive. What year was this?

2 Approximately how many millions of acres of forestland are there in Maine?

3 The King's Broad Arrow on the trunk of a white pine signified that tree's selection for use by the English Royal Navy. The mark of the arrow indicated that the trunk of the tree was a minimum of how many inches in diameter?

4 Portland was the first capital of Maine and state legislators met in that city from 1820 until the new State Capitol at Augusta was completed in 1832. But in what year was Augusta officially voted to be the capital of Maine?

5 How many years ago did the great sheets of glacial ice retreat from the Maine shoreline?

6 How many of Maine's counties have Indian names?

7 Each of the following Maine communities holds an annual festival associated with a Maine food product. Name the product for each town.
   Yarmouth   Houlton   Oxford   Belfast   Rockland

8 More festivals. Again, match the product with the towns.
   Pittsfield   Machias   South Berwick   Fort Fairfield
   Winter Harbor

Answers to Pens-In-Hand

1 1919.

James G. Blaine died in 1893. In 1919, his family donated the Blaine mansion to the state as an official residence for the governor. Carl E. Milliken was the first governor to reside in this magnificant, 28-room structure, (plus nine baths and nine fireplaces), which is located directly across the street from the State House.

2 About 17 million acres.

Maine is the most heavily forested state in the country. In 1979, the total timber cut in Maine was 5,396,232 cords, which was 17 percent above the ten year average of 4,607,953 cords. The largest cut was from Aroostook County, followed by Piscataquis, Somerset and Washington. Of the exact figure of 17,748,000 acres, 16,894,300 acres are commercial forest, owned by about 100,000 landowners. Some 50 percent of the annual cut comes from owners of under 5,000 acres each.

3 24 inches.

It was measured a foot from the ground. The 1691 provision in the Massachusetts charter that decreed this practice caused great controversy in the colonies. The law was often evaded, with the connivance of local judges. It was supposedly a 100-pound fine if you were caught with an illegal "mast tree."

4 1827.

The removal of the capital to Augusta from Portland occasioned fierce controversy. Augusta was first selected in 1822, but stalling tactics by Portland legislators delayed a definitive move until 1827 when a vote was taken in behalf of Augusta, but leaving the Legislature to meet in Portland — a maneuver that Portland supported in the hope of delaying the inevitable. As late as 1907, Portland was still trying to have the capital moved back.

5 12,000 years ago.

6 Six.

Androscoggin, Aroostook, Kennebec, Penobscot, Piscataquis, Sagadahoc.

7 Yarmouth — **clam**
Houlton — **potato**
Oxford — **beanhole bean**
Belfast — **broiler**
Rockland — **seafood**

8 Pittsfield — **egg**
Machias — **blueberry**
South Berwick — **strawberry**
Fort Fairfield — **potato**
Winter Harbor — **lobster**

Visual Questions 3

1 She wrote her most famous book while living in Brunswick, Maine. Earlier she had lived in Cincinnati with her professor husband and had witnessed at close-hand some of the evils of slavery. Her brother was a famous New England minister of the gospel and her father had also been a clergyman. Identify this famous woman pictured here.

2 The lady pictured here was a resident of Gardiner, Maine, and also a well-known writer. Her mother was Julia Ward Howe, who wrote "The Battle Hymn of the Republic" and her father was Dr. Samuel Gridley Howe, who founded the Perkins Institute for the Blind in Boston. Her own most widely read book is *Captain January*, the story of a lighthouse keeper and his adopted daughter, which has been made into two movies. Identify her.

3 Also a resident of Gardiner, Maine, was the male writer who can be found in this picture. He wasn't born in Gardiner, but in the tiny village of Head Tide. *The Man Against the Sky* was the title of his first successful book of poetry. He won the Pulitzer Prize for his work. Once you have located him in the photograph, identify him.

Answers to Visual Questions

1 Harriet Beecher Stowe.

Mrs. Stowe came to Maine in 1850 when her husband Calvin E. Stowe was named Professor of Biblical Literature at Bowdoin.

In February, 1851, while attending church services in Brunswick, Mrs. Stowe had a sudden vision that translated itself into the inspiration for *Uncle Tom's Cabin*. It was a vision of the death of an aged slave. She had written books before, but only of a religious or philosophical nature. Her powerful first novel was written in the Stowe home on Federal Street, partly on brown wrapping paper when she ran out of regular writing paper.

Henry Ward Beecher, the renowned Congregational preacher of Brooklyn, New York, and eloquent anti-slavery leader, was her brother and both were the children of the Reverand Lyman Beecher of Connecticut. Among Mrs. Stowe's later works was a novel set in Maine, *Pearl of Orr's Island*.

2 Laura Richards.

Laura Elizabeth Howe Richards was the author of 80 books, most of them for children, and also the hostess in her Gardiner home for anyone with a desire to discuss literature — a sort of Down East "Salon" where such notables in letters as Alexander Woolcott, Conrad Aiken, Ogden Nash and Edward Arlington Robinson might be seen, as well as any number of local people, including high school students.

Mrs. Richards, collaborating with her sister, Maud Howe Elliott, won a Pulitzer prize in 1917 for a biography of her mother. She wrote other biographies by herself of notable women and was active in many charitable causes.

3 Edwin Arlington Robinson.

Robinson left Gardiner, where he grew up, to go to Harvard and three years after he left Cambridge, published his first volume of verse, *The Torrent and the Night Before* at his own expense. This was in 1896. It was not until 1916 that he finally achieved any significant recognition. Meanwhile, however, he had been helped by Theodore Roosevelt who had found him a job at the New York Customs House and by the MacDowell Colony in Peterborough, New Hampshire. At the time of Robinson's death in 1935, he was considered America's finest poet. His portraits of individuals like Miniver Cheevy, Richard Cory, Reuben Bright, Luke Havergal in Tilbury Town (Gardiner) are among his most remembered works.

4 Below are outline maps of three of Maine's counties. They are in the south, the center and the north of the State, but not necessarily in that order. Identify them.

a.

b.

c.

5 Paul Bunyan, pictured in the statue at right, is a legendary lumberjack more closely associated in the public mind with Michigan and the Middle West. Yet Maine has claims on him, too, and the city that has erected this giant statue of him has, in the past, declared itself "the lumbering capital of the world." In what Maine city will you find the statue of Paul Bunyan?

6 Whitewater rafting has in recent years become a popular sport and a good-sized business in Maine. One of the most important areas for rafting is the West Branch of the Penobscot River at the so-called "Big-A" site. On what other river in Maine is there even more white water rafting activity?

4 a. York County, b. Androscoggin County, c. Penobscot County.

a.

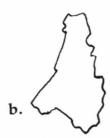

b.

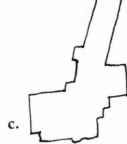

c.

5 Bangor.

Bangor claims that Bunyan was born within its environs on February 12, 1834. The date happens to be the same day on which the "Queen City" was incorporated. It is said that Bunyan left the state for the west when Maine ran out of tall pine for him to cut. Bunyan's prize possession was his blue ox, Babe. Between his horns he measured 42 ax handles and a plug of tobacco.

6 The Kennebec.

On the upper Kennebec, above The Forks at Harris Dam, is the starting point for a 12 and a half mile run that is the most frequented of Maine's white water rafting trips. A proposed dam has threatened the Big A site of the Penobscot. The white water rafting industry, which has grown phenomenally in Maine, is now estimated to be worth $5–$10 million a year.

Essay Questions

SHILOH

Religious originality has not been lacking in Maine. Various sects from the 18th century Sandemanians or Glassites in southern York County to the Shakers at Sabbathday Lake have taken root in the state. None have been more interesting or controversial than the cult founded by Bowdoin graduate Frank W. Sandford at the beginning of the 20th century. Several names have been ascribed to it. Its official title was the Kingdom, Incorporated. More popularly, it was referred to as The Holy Ghost and Us Society or simply Sandfordism. But the catch-all term for the religious community that Sandford formed was Shiloh, the name he gave to the commune-type establishment that he built atop a hill in Durham.

It was quite a place in its heyday. The dormitories had space for 500 converts. There was a hospital, a playhouse for children, a number of communal halls and a main administration building topped by a five-story tower known as the Eye of the Needle, on which a domed and gilded cupola advertised Shiloh's presence to the world.

Sandford, a native of Bowdoinham, once had been a semi-professional baseball player. As a Baptist minister, he discovered his charismatic talents for preaching and soon set off on his own path by forming a select group in which he was known as Elijah. He commanded unquestioning obedience and had his followers turn over all of their material possessions to him.

At Shiloh, hundreds of people from throughout the world, including a Japanese lady, an African prince and a wealthy Texan, labored from morn to night, ate plain meals and foreswore smoking, drinking, dancing, and any other frivolity.

In 1911, Sandford announced the impending end of the world and named the day and hour. When nothing happened, his credibility was a bit shaken — but only a bit. The quick-witted Sandford announced that God had been touched by the prayers of the faithful at Shiloh and had decided to spare the world for further proselytizing by the Kingdom. With a mysterious $10,000 check, Sandford then purchased a yacht and put to sea with 45 cult members as crew. Off they went to the Holy Land then to Africa and then all over the world on a quixotic and disastrous voyage. Eight crew members died of scurvy and malnutrition in the course of it.

When he returned to the United States, Sandford was prosecuted for manslaughter and also for kidnapping (since he had held a woman cult member aboard against her will). He spent two years at the federal penitentiary in Atlanta. Released, he disappeared behind the walls at Shiloh. Rumors still persist that he remains alive there ready to resume leadership of the sect.

---

1. *Where was Frank W. Sandford born?*

2. *Where did he locate Shiloh?*

3. *How many converts could Shiloh's dormitories hold?*

4. *How many of his crew members died?*

5. *How many years did he spend in federal prison?*

---

1. **Bowdoinham.**

2. **Durham.**

3. **500.**

4. **Eight.**

5. **Two.**

The tower at Shiloh, the controversial religious community founded by Frank Sandford.

A rare photo of Frank Sandford and some of his followers.

William Pitt Fessenden, the U.S. senator from Maine who committed political suicide by voting against the impeachment of President Andrew Johnson.

President Lyndon Baines Johnson on his campaign visit to Portland in 1964.

Sarah Orne Jewett, daughter of a South Berwick physician, one of Maine's most renowned writers of fiction.

An artist's view of Bangor in the heyday of its lumbering career.

Maine's State bird — the black-capped chickadee.

The Franklin Delano Roosevelt summer home at Campobello, now part of an international park.

Maine's State flower — the white pine cone and tassel.

Maine's State animal — the moose.

What You Ought to Know About Maine

ARTS AND LETTERS

It has been remarked that in addition to potatoes and fish, Maine exports books about Maine."

So states the article on Maine in the 1963 edition of the Columbia Encyclopedia. The article then lists a roster of literary luminaries that would do honor to many a country, never mind a small, isolated New England state: names like Sarah Orne Jewett, Edward Arlington Robinson, Robert P. Tristram Coffin, Edna St. Vincent Millay, Mary Ellen Chase, Kenneth Roberts and Kate Douglas Wiggins.

Many other names can be added — distinguished authors who wrote prior to these above mentioned literary figures of the late 19th and early 20th centuries, and also the distinguished writers who are presently at work in Maine.

Nor is Maine's attraction to the creative spirit, confined to those who deal with the written word. Maine is equally celebrated for the painters who live and have lived here, as well as the musicians who have called Maine their home.

The cultural heritage of Maine is sweeping in scope. Here are some of the highlights.

Literature

America's first female novelist was born Sally Sayward Barrell in York, Maine. Some of her works that began appearing shortly after 1800 were signed "A Lady of Maine" or "A Lady of Massachusetts", but it was as "Madam Wood" after her marriage to General Abiel Wood, that she was best known. The literary merit of her pioneer work may be debated, but she was the first to preach the necessity for an "American" literature, rather than a slavish copying of English style. *Julia and the Illuminated Baron*, *Amelia* and *Tales of Night*, were the titles of some of her romances.

It is not known if Portland-born John Neal was following Madam Wood's advice when he too began espousing the cause of an "American" literature in the early 19th century. However, Neal is credited with being the first to recognize and expound Edgar Allen Poe's unique talents to audiences beyond America, as well as to acquaint those audiences with the developing American literature of the time.

Neal himself was a writer and he used a particular American idiom, setting his stories in America, using rough American language and avoiding the imitation of the more genteel British authors. In England, in 1824 and 1825, he wrote a series of articles for *Blackwood's Magazine* describing America's writers. Back in Maine, in 1827, Neal had to defend himself physically against some of his fellow citizens angered at the "kiss and tell" revelations he had made in his expose novel about Portland called *Keep Cool*. Among the books he published while in England was one called *Brother Jonathan* or *The New Englanders*. "Brother Jonathan", of course, during this era, was a nickname for Americans.

The Class of 1825, at Bowdoin included Henry Wadsworth Longfellow and Nathaniel Hawthorne among its graduates, in addition to Franklin Pierce, later President of the United States. Longfellow may well be deemed the most illustrious and popular poet that Maine has ever produced; Hawthorne, while not strictly a Maine writer, could certainly be considered the most talented prose writer ever to have been influenced by the state. At least one of his stories, *The Minister's Black Veil*, derives directly from an incident that occurred in Maine and the thesis has been advanced that a model for the house in the *House of the Seven Gables* was to be found in Maine in General Henry Knox's home at Thomaston and not in Salem, Massachusetts where the story is set.

Another Massachusetts writer who found subject matter in Maine and Maine history was John Greenleaf Whittier, who also spent his summers in the state. His long poem, *Mogg Megone*, tells the story of the 1724 raid on Norridgewock and

Maud Muller is another famous poem that developed from an experience Whittier had in the vicinity of what is still known as "Maud Muller Spring" in York.

Harriet Beecher Stowe's immortal contribution to American literature, written in Maine, has already been discussed. After the Civil War Maine became the site of almost a literary colony as a whole group of distinguished writers came to summer or settle here. Some of lasting reputation like Mark Twain were merely steady visitors; others like William Dean Howells, the champion of the realistic novel, stayed. Maine's own Sarah Orne Jewett began writing her incomparable stories of Maine life for a national readership. Celia Thaxter, out on the Isles of Shoals, wrote splendid poetry. Writers who were popular at the time, like Finley Peter Dunne, the political satirist and creator of "Mr. Dooley" (a latter-day "Artemus Ward") or Thomas Nelson Page, the southern novelist-diplomat, had vacation homes here. On a purely local note, William R. Pattangall was writing in the Down East vein of humor that had directly descended from Seba Smith in the previous century. Fanny Hardy Eckstrom at the same time was penning her interesting regional studies of the Maine north woods.

As the 20th century advanced, Maine saw the blossoming of a number of its own literary sons and daughters, like Edna St. Vincent Millay, Edward Arlington Robinson and Robert P. Tristram Coffin — all Pulitzer Prize winners — as was Kennebunk's Kenneth Roberts, a former journalist who retired to Maine to write magnificent historical novels that reflected the state's eventful past. Popular writers like Laura Richards, Kate Douglas Wiggins, Mary Ellen Chase, Louise Dickinson Rich, Gladys Hasty Carroll and Booth Tarkington, writing on his yacht anchored off Kennebunkport, were also most prolific. Ben Ames Williams, in his *Fraternity Village*, vividly and successfully recreated the life of a small Waldo County town.

In the present day, Maine is still home to a number of noted American writers and even to one of the most famous contemporary French writers, Marguerite Yourcenar, the first woman ever elected to the prestigious Academie Française. Although she writes only in French, Madame Yourcenar has made her home in Northeast Harbor since 1950. Another transplanted author who has put down strong roots in Maine is E.B. White — Elwyn Brooks White — the dean of *New Yorker Magazine* writers and creator of two delightful young people's classics with a decidedly Maine flavor, *Charlotte's Web* and *Stuart Little*. The children's story itself as a genre, has a long tradition in Maine, back to Jacob Abbott and Elijah Kellogg, and forward to Robert McCloskey, the prize-winning author of *Blueberries for Sal*. One of America's most important contemporary women writers — May Sarton — is a year-round resident of Maine. And not only a resident but a native is the master of the horror story — the best-selling Stephen King. The creator of the novel behind the popular TV series "M.A.S.H." — Richard Hooker (a nom de plume) — is a doctor in Waterville and has even written a *M.A.S.H. Goes to Maine* volume, and the widely-read Dutch mystery writer, Janwillem Van de Wetering has set one of his brooding murder mystery novels in Maine.

If Maine had a literary trophy wall, it would be stacked with Pulitzer Prizes and other honors — a proud tradition of inspiration to writers that shows no sign of lessening.

Painting and Sculpture

Maine's own "Renaissance Man" of the late 1700's and early 1800's Jonathan Fisher, was one of the first painters in the state. He did not consider his portraits, landscapes, still-lifes and drawings of plants and animals of particular importance, given the wide range of activities in which this remarkable preacher of Blue Hill was engaged. An inventor, farmer, educational reformer, theologian and much else besides, he was also a fine enough artist so that a one-man show of his works at Rockland in 1967 drew 20,000 spectators.

By 1829, John Neal, something of a "Renaissance Man" himself — writer, secretary to the world-famous philosopher Jeremy Bentham and miniaturist painter — was writing the following about the condition of the visual arts in America:

"We have certainly, either by nature . . . or by accident, something that appears like a decided predisposition for painting in this country . . . painters, if not too numerous to mention are much too numerous to particularize. They are . . . more than we know what to do with . . ."

As regards Maine, it is not certain to whom Neal was referring. John Adams Bartlett (1817–1902) of Rumford was an important early primitive portrait painter, but his works weren't really discovered until 1976. Perhaps Neal had in mind William Matthew Prior of Bath and Portland whose idol was Gilbert Stuart and whose portraits sometimes reflected Stuart's influence, or Prior's brother-in-law, Sturtevant J. Hamblin of Portland, a talented portraitist. Rufus Porter, America's first important mural painter, also travelled in the state and spent a short time in Denmark, Maine, decorating sleighs.

The one Maine artist known to have a definite connection with John Neal was Harrison Bird Brown who did landscape paintings. Actually, Brown preferred doing portraits to landscapes and was not successful at it until one day the sharp-tongued Neal, on a visit to his studio, advised him to stop wasting time on portraits. With his seascapes of Casco Bay and his views of the White Mountains, as well as some European and Canadian scenes, Brown became popular, especially so during the 1860's and 1870's.

Thomas Cole, Thomas Doughty, Frederick Edwin Church and Fitz Hugh Lane are American painters of the pre-Civil War period who came to Maine to paint, although their roots lay elsewhere. Cole, as the leader of the "Hudson River School," is the most noted. Mount Desert Island was a particular magnet for them, while Lane, normally associated with Gloucester, Massachusetts and called "the first marine painter of real stature in America", also did a picture of Owl's Head and a well known canvas entitled, "Twilight On the Kennebec."

Winslow Homer was a war correspondent artist during the Civil War. Essentially an illustrator, he went abroad to study art and after a stay in Tynemouth, England on the North Sea, changed his style and technique. Back in America, he decided that he wanted to live by the sea and he chose Prout's Neck, a part of Scarborough. There he fully developed into the great artist that he became — possibly the greatest who ever worked in Maine. For 27 years, until his death, he rarely left Prout's Neck, and then only for short trips, mostly fishing and hunting excursions. Fittingly, Homer died in his Prout's Neck studio on September 29, 1910.

The year before, a 32-year-old Maine artist from Lewiston had his first exhibition in New York City. It was thanks to his friend, the photographer Alfred Stieglitz, that Marsden Hartley was able to show his works at Stieglitz's Photo Secession Gallery. For 30 years afterward, Hartley travelled and exhibited in Europe where he received more recognition than in the United States.

He came home to Maine in 1939 and settled in Corea near Winter Harbor. The next year his picture "End of the Hurricane, Lane's Island, Maine," won a prestigious prize in Philadelphia. A poet as well as a painter, Hartley also expressed Maine themes in his written works, one of which was called "Androscoggin."

Since his death in 1943, Hartley's place among American painters has continued to grow, capped by the monumental showing of more than 100 of his works at the Whitney Museum in New York City in 1980.

Other artists of note who worked in Maine during these years include John Marin, famed for his modernistic seascapes; Walt Kuhn, the incomparable painter of circus clowns; N.C. Wyeth and Rockwell Kent, the illustrators; and Robert Laurent, the sculptor.

Several famous sculptors have strong ties to Maine. William Zorach was born in Lithuania and came to America at age four. In 1923 he and his American-born wife, Marguerite Thompson Zorach, herself an artist, settled in Maine in the Georgetown area. Commissions for William's work came from the U.S. Post Office in Washington D.C. and Radio City Music Hall in New York City, as well as from nearby Bath for its town park. The couple's daughter, Dahlov Ipcar, carries on the family's artistic tradition and is noted for her colorful animal scenes.

Also from Eastern Europe came another renowned Maine sculptor, Louise Nevelson (Nee Berliawsky, in Kiev, Russia), brought to Rockland at the age of five. She married Charles

Nevelson after a typical Maine upbringing in Rockland where she was captain of the girls' basketball team and vice president of the glee club. It was not until 1958 when she was nearly 60 years old that Louise Nevelson finally achieved recognition. Her exhibition called "Moon Garden + One" at the Museum of Modern Art in New York was an overnight sensation. Now past 80, she has been honored by some of the most important museums in the country. Her work is almost entirely in wood, which it could be claimed, may have some subliminal connection with her Maine upbringing.

Artists of all sorts continue to flock to Maine and to be inspired by the state and its people, none more so than Andrew Wyeth, the most successful of modern American painters. He divides his time between Cushing, Maine and Chadd's Ford, Pennsylvania. Two of his most famous paintings, "Christina's World" and "The Patriot" were done in Maine with Maine models. His artist son, Jamie, also spends considerable time in Maine, as did his own father, N.C. Wyeth.

Music

Portland, Maine is the smallest city in the United States to have a full-time symphony orchestra. The venerable tradition of the P.S.O. and its continued support by the local citizenry is a reflection of a long-standing reverence for serious music among Maine people.

It is interesting to note that the full name of Cyris Curtis, the Portland-born publishing magnate who owned the *Saturday Evening Post*, was Cyris Herman Kotzschmar Curtis, his two middle names taken from the 19th century organist-composer Herman Kotzschmar who had been a friend of Curtis's father. In 1912, Curtis had the Kotzschmar Memorial Organ installed in Portland's City Hall Auditorium to honor his namesake. The $60,000 organ had been ordered from a Hartford, Connecticut manufacturer with the stipulation that it be "as nearly perfect in every respect as possible." As a result of Curtis's gift, Portland became the first city in America to hire a municipal organist — William C. MacFarlane, the composer of "America the Beautiful." Curtis also later bought organs for Bowdoin College and two churches in Camden.

One of Herman Kotzschmar's students in Portland was John Knowles Paine, who has been called America's "first serious composer of rank." After studying music in Germany, Paine gravitated to Harvard University where he built the music department from scratch and was the first occupant of a Chair of Music at an American university.

Meanwhile, Paine also composed. His music was performed in Germany at the Wagner Festival and in America in 1873, his "Saint Peter" was the first oratorio by an American composer ever to be performed in this country. Appropriately enough, it was done in Portland. He was commissioned to write a piece for the nation's centennial celebration in 1876 and had numerous works played by the Boston Symphony. He was for many years Harvard's official organist. He has often been referred to as "The Father of American Music" and "The Dean of American Composers."

Walter Piston followed in his footsteps. Born in Rockland in 1894 (twelve years before Paine's death), Piston went to Harvard, also taught there, became a full professor in 1944, and in 1948 became the University's first Walter W. Naumberg Professor of Music.

Like Paine, Piston composed while he taught. In all, he completed eight symphonies, five string quartets, a ballet and several concerti. Two of his symphonies won Pulitzer Prizes and he was also the recipient of numerous other awards.

Piston often returned to Maine. His "Pine Tree Fantasy," recalling his boyhood in Rockland, was premiered by the Portland Symphony Orchestra in 1965 and his last work in 1976 "Concerto for String Quartet, Winds and Percussion" was dedicated to the Portland String Quartet.

Other talented musicians linked to the state include Lillian Nordica, the famous operatic soprano of the late 19th century, born Lillian Norton in Farmington; Emma Eames, another talented operatic soprano of world-wide reputation who grew up in Bath; Robert Browne Hall, the composer of many military marches, including one played at the funeral of President

John F. Kennedy; and Pierre Monteux, the distinguished conductor of numerous symphony orchestras here and abroad, who made his home in Hancock, Maine. It is said of Monteux, who received about every honor possible for a musician, that one of his proudest accomplishments was to be named honorary fire chief of the Hancock Volunteer Fire Department and it was in this capacity that he once attended an international gathering of fire-fighters.

The Monteux-inspired annual music festival in tiny Hancock — like the highly acclaimed Skowhegan School of Painting, America's foremost summer art school — are but the tip of the iceberg in any overall picture of the state of the arts in Maine. The recent opening of a "world-class" refurbished Portland Museum of Art that drew attention all over the country is but another example of where Maine stands. The Brunswick Summer Music Festival, the Portland Art School, the Monmouth Shakespeare Theatre, the Farnsworth Museum in Rockland — these and many other arts organizations continue to gain in strength, aided by an effective State Commission on the Arts and Humanities and a sympathetic State Legislature. The latter has voted that a percentage of the cost of every public building in Maine be devoted to the purchase of works of art and has even statutorily made it possible for the widow of the late sculptor Bernard Langlais to settle the taxes on his estate by donating several of his sculptures.

If the image of Maine occasionally tends to be that of a cold, isolated, rural, forested northern land of backcountry, folksy people, a closer look for anyone who knows the facts shows a deep sophistication here in literature, painting, music, theatre, etc. — a displaced "urbanism," one might say, without the problems associated with big city life. Maine's position vis a vis arts and letters has been and remains a vital one.

Kenneth Roberts, famed for his historic novels based on Maine's past.

Louise Nevelson, Rockland-born, internationally known for her highly individualistic and distinctive sculptures.

"Shipping in Down East Waters" by Fitz Hugh Lane (1804–65)

"A Morning View of Blue Hill Village, 1829" by Jonathan Fisher (1768–1847)

*"Monhegan, Maine" by
Rockwell Kent (1882–1971)*

"Maine Coast at Vinalhaven" by Marsden Hartley (1877–1943)

What You Ought to Know About Maine

MAINE PEOPLE

It is always somewhat of a problem to know exactly what to call a citizen of the State of Maine. A Texan is always a Texan, a Californian a Californian. But a person from Maine can be a "Mainer", even, somewhat seriously, a "Mainiac," or a "Downeaster". Yet over and above this confusion of terms is another one that the people of Maine employ to describe themselves. It is a little bit of an "in" term, something that comes to natives naturally. They call themselves "Maine people".

Maine people come in all shapes and sizes. They come in all ethnic hues, even though certain ancestries seem predominant. The background of Maine people is first and foremost English. Descendants of the early settlers who spread through the state from more southerly regions (i.e., Massachusetts), they can be found everywhere in Maine today. In some areas, their heavy concentration imparts a special flavor, like the so-called "Bible belt" around Houlton in southern Aroostook County where the Anglo-Saxon, fundamentalist overtones are reminiscent of the Deep South or the Middle West.

Next in numbers come the Franco-Americans. Their enclaves are in the northern reaches of Aroostook County — the St. John Valley — and in certain of the mill towns, notably Lewiston, Biddeford, Sanford, Waterville and Augusta.

Significant concentrations of Americans of Irish descent are to be found in Portland and Bangor and these cities, too, contain the state's larger groupings of people of Italian and Eastern European Jewish origin.

Many small ethnic pockets exist: Lebanese in Waterville: Greeks in Saco: Finns in South Paris: Swedes in Aroostook

County: Slovaks in the Lisbon area: the Germans around Broadbay in Knox County who came in the 1700's: Scots who were brought as prisoners of war in the 1600's: even the post World War II influx of Russians and Ukrainians to Richmond. There are small numbers of blacks and apparently a slightly larger Hispanic population. The Indians — the Penobscots, Passamaquoddies, Malecites and assorted others — have always had an impact on the consciousness of the state far disproportionate to their small numbers.

Thus Maine is a melting pot as much as any other part of the nation despite the "Yankee" aura that its name connotes. Those who live here and work here know this.

Many illustrious Americans have sprung from the Down East soil. These famous figures are easy to work into questions and answers: Henry Wadsworth Longfellow, Hannibal Hamlin, Edmund S. Muskie, Margaret Chase Smith. Through the years Maine has continued to turn out sons and daughters who become nationally important to their time.

But there are hundred of others who are not so well known and yet who deserve to be cited. Some of them, too, have already appeared on these pages — Chester Greenwood and his ear muffs; Alden Pulsifer, the wandering postmaster and his dogsled; Captain Samuel Clough, the rescuer-*manqué* of Marie Antoinette.

Following now, pretty much at random, but in keeping with the idea of What You Ought to Know About Maine, or rather, Who You Should Know in Maine, are some other interesting Maine people who have enriched the state and its reputation, each in his or her own individual fashion.

An individualist among the individualists in the craggy, independent style of Mainers who speak their minds, (even when they sometimes change them) was William Robinson Pattangall, the lawyer-writer from Down East in Washington County who eventually became the chief justice of the Maine Supreme Judicial Court.

Pattangall is best remembered for his political satire as embodied in his books, *The Meddybemps Letters* and *The Maine Hall of Fame*. At the time (the early 1900's), Pattangall was a legislator (serving first from Machias and later from Waterville) and a Democrat, in an age when political control of Maine was firmly in the hands of the Republican Party. Pattangall's witty thrusts and gibes were at the personalities and practices of the ruling Republicans and, as the well-known Lewiston editor Arthur G. Staples wrote, "They began to undermine the very foundation of Republican Party domination. . . . For the first time, the sacred careers of the great were dissected by simple humor." Pattangall's irony was all the more tart, perhaps, since he had recently defected from the G.O.P. to join the Democrats.

Meddybemps (population 110 in 1980) is a small village near Pembroke (1980 population 922) where Pattengall was born. In the *Meddybemps Letters*, following the tradition set by Seba Smith in the *Major Jack Downing Letters*, the lampooning of current events was done by a fictional character — in this case Stephen A. Douglas Smith, a Meddybemps plow salesman. His "letters" dealt with conflicts-of-interest, ineptitude and even graft within the ruling circles.

Pattangall's notoriety and popularity led him to be the Democrats' (unsuccessful) candidate for governor in 1922 and in 1924. Maverick that he was, he later went back to the Republican Party, in which, always the non-conformist, he led an attack on the Ku Klux Klan, then powerful in Maine and supported by some Republican luminaries.

Pattangall was attorney general of Maine several times. Governor William Tudor Gardiner appointed him chief justice of the Maine Supreme Judicial Court in 1931. His name was mentioned for the U.S. Supreme Court on several occasions. Born in 1865, he died in 1942, an eloquent voice in Maine public life for more than half a century.

In 1875, James Augustine Healy was named bishop of the Roman Catholic Diocese of Portland and thus, in effect, the spiritual head of the 80,000 Catholics in Maine and New Hampshire. At first blush, there seemed nothing extraordinary in the naming of a person with an Irish surname to be in charge of the region's Catholics. Most of the leaders of the Church in America in that day were of Irish descent.

But there was something different about Bishop Healy. His father was Irish. His mother, however, had been a black slave and by the racial standards of the time Healy himself was considered black. Raised on his father's plantation in Georgia, he went north for his education and was graduated from Holy Cross in 1849. He was ordained a priest in 1854.

Healy was the first black bishop in the history of the American Catholic Church. The assignment of northern New England was, to put it mildly, a difficult post for him. First, he was only the second Catholic bishop in an area where anti-Catholic feeling had always been strong and where there had even been riots against the Catholics. Second, Healy was a black and prejudice against blacks was rampant.

And yet, Bishop Healy more than proved himself. Through tact, concern, devotion to his flock, charity and great energy, he won over the people in his charge. He endured ostracism and ignorance. And he did so with grace. To a young girl who once called him "black as the devil", he gently replied, "You can say I'm as black as coal or black as the Ace of Spades, but, please dear, don't say I'm black as the devil".

Bishop James Healy, son of an Irish immigrant and a black slave, bishop of Maine, and the first black bishop in the history of the American Roman Catholic Church.

During his tenure, which lasted until his death in 1900, Healy added 66 churches, 21 schools, 68 missions and numerous convents to his diocese, as well as providing organized welfare and a constant, living lesson in tolerance.

Born in Hampden and raised in Maine was Dorothea Dix, later to win a world-wide reputation for her one-woman crusade to reform penal institutions and the treatment of the mentally ill. Her family's long association with Maine, which began when her grandfather purchased a vast tract of wilderness from Bowdoin College, is commemorated in the names of two contemporary Maine towns — Dixmont and Dixfield.

As a teacher in the Boston area, she was shocked into action after visiting a jail in East Cambridge and finding mentally retarded and mentally ill persons thrown in the same cells with hardened criminals. From then on, she campaigned tirelessly not only in the United States but even in Russia and Japan for changes in penal and other institutional systems. She even enlisted the help of Pope Pius IX after having an audience with him. During the Civil War, she served as superintendant of nurses for the Union Army.

Through Dorothea Dix's efforts, both before and after the War, state hospitals for the mentally ill were established. Ironically, it was in one of these hospitals — the Trenton, New Jersey Insane Asylum, which she entered for treatment in the 1880's when her health failed — that she died. She never married. Yet in 1969, a cache of letters — purported to be "love letters" from her — were found in a vacant mansion in New York State. They were to ex-President Millard Fillmore, at the time a widower, but their content has never been revealed.

In 1910, Congress approved $10,000 for a memorial to her in Hampden.

Lillian Nordica was another Maine woman of distinction in an era when it was difficult for women to make their way in the world. She was born Lillian Norton in Farmington. Blessed with a beautiful singing voice, she studied opera in Milan, where she made her debut in 1879. Not until 1883 did she sing in America, after successful European performances in Paris, London and St. Petersburg. In 1890, she first sang at the Metropolitan Opera House in New York City. After going to Bayreuth, Germany in 1894, she added Wagner to her repertory, which included roles like that of Marguerite in "Faust" and it was as a Wagnerian soprano that she was most famous. The Nordica Homestead Museum, her birthplace in Farmington, contains her concert gowns, stage jewels, programs from the operas in which she sang, music and other memorabilia connected with this internationally renowned diva from Franklin County.

Portrait of Lillian Nordica, born Lillian Norton in Farmington, who achieved world-wide fame as an operatic soprano.

In 1638, John Josselyn came to Maine to be with his brother Henry at Black Point. Henry was soon to be appointed deputy governor of Maine in those beginning days of colonization when Maine was ruled under the King's grant to Sir Ferdinando Gorges. Later, Henry Josselyn was to be the first and only Royal Chief Justice of Maine, but it was John — already quoted with regard to passenger pigeons — who has achieved a more lasting memory through his writings. John Josselyn was Maine's first naturalist and in his book *New England Rarities* are some of the earliest and best accounts of New England Botany.

Other titles by John Josselyn, containing valuable data and descriptions, include *An Account of Two Voyages made to New England, 1638, and 1663* and *A perfect Description of an Indian Squaw in all her Bravery: with a Poem not improperly conferr'd upon her*. The latter work has Josselyn's oft-quoted sardonic line about Indians that "the only tame cattle they possess are dogs and lice".

Baron Munchausen had nothing on John Josselyn. He told some amazing whoppers, like the one about the sea serpent that appeared off Cape Ann, sunning itself on the rocks, "coiled up like a shippe cable", or the tale already told here of Michael Mitton chopping off a merman's hand (Josselyn also called the beast a triton).

Of such tales as these, or of witches' orgies along the Maine coast beheld by witnesses, Josselyn states that he is merely repeating what he's heard. "The credit whereof I will neither impeach nor enforce", adds this initial practitioner in the great tradition of Maine storytelling.

A storyteller of a different sort was John Ford, one of Hollywood's most honored film directors and the man credited with having elevated the western to a work of art in such movies as *Stagecoach*, *The Horse Soldiers* and *Cheyenne Autumn*.

Born in Portland as Sean Aloysius O'Feeny, the future moviemaker was a star running back and defensive lineman on the Portland High School football team and then left his family's home on Munjoy Hill to join an older brother in Hollywood. It was here that he changed his name and, after a brief stint as an actor, he began to direct films.

He won four Oscars for feature films he directed plus two more for documentaries made during World War II. He was credited with having discovered John Wayne and used him in many movies. For 52 years, Ford worked in Hollywood, putting out one major film after another.

He often returned to Maine to visit his mother, donated to charities in Maine (particularly those of veterans' organizations) and, in turn was made a lifelong member of Portland's Harold T. Andrews VFW Post. He was retired from the service as a Navy rear admiral and died in 1973 at the age of 77.

In the summer of 1903, playing shortstop for the Boston Red Sox, Freddy Parent was called the "Flying Frenchman" — because "fly" he did that season, leading the Red Sox to the pennant with a burst of energy in the final 30 games. Parent batted .350, knocked in runs, stole bases — and then pretty much did the same in the World Series to beat the Pittsburgh Pirates of Honus Wagner after they had established a 3-1 lead in games.

Born in Biddeford, migrating to Sanford to work in the Goodall Mills at age 16, Parent played on the town team and on semi-pro teams until he finally ended up in Boston in the newly formed American League. He was in the majors for 11 years, with Boston and then the Chicago White Sox. His career batting average was a more than respectable .262 and he played in a total of 1,129 games.

It was reputedly Parent, in later years, while playing with the then minor league Baltimore Orioles, who advised the Red Sox to sign up a promising young teammate of his named Babe Ruth. At the age of 55, Freddy Parent was still playing semi-pro ball and he claimed his greatest thrill ever was to get a hit at the age of 75 in an Irish-French charity game in Lewiston. He was made a charter member of the Maine Sports Hall of Fame before his death at the age of 95.

Among the Acadian French of the St. John Valley in the uppermost regions of Maine, the people of Madawaska still cherish the memory of Marguerite Blanche Thibodeau Cyr, known as "Tante Blanche," (Aunt Blanche), the heroine of the colony's bleakest days in the late 18th century. A "Tante Blanche Historic Museum" is today maintained by the Madawaska Historical Society.

It was in 1797 that disaster almost overtook the 30 or so families established in Madawaska. Two years of floods, September frosts and heavy snowstorms had destroyed the crops so that *la grande disette* or *la misere noire*, both meaning "the great famine", had descended on the small community. Some people left for New Brunswick, but those who stayed lived on dwindling supplies that eventually ran out. Throughout their hardships, Tante Blanche proved to be their saving strength, visiting them all on snowshoes, buoying their spirits, tending the sick, burying the dead, providing whatever resources she could until help finally came.

For years afterward, she played an important role in the community, highly respected and even venerated. On her mother's side she was descended from René Leblanc, the notary of Grand-Pré in Nova Scotia, from whence the Acadians were expelled, and who is mentioned in Longfellow's epic poem about that tragedy, *Evangeline*.

The Indians of Maine have produced many notable personages. Chief Neptune of the Penobscots was the subject of an interesting book by Fanny Hardy Eckstrom, Maine's fine historian of the north woods. It is an intriguing work because in it Chief Neptune becomes an almost mystical folk-hero, like Glooskap, although he was also a real flesh and blood person and neighbor of Mrs. Eckstrom's in Old Town.

John Neptune was called a great *m'teoulino*, meaning shaman or wizard. He was credited with magical powers, such as being able to make his voice heard one hundred miles away, or being able to find green corn in winter, or tobacco in the forest. His powers, it was claimed, were learned from the Chippewas in the West. In one epic story, he was pictured as transforming himself into a giant eel in order to fight the dread underwater lake monster, "Wiwiliamecq," and after defeating it, changing back into himself but still smelling like a fish.

Neptune was the "Old Governor" whom Henry David Thoreau met on his trip to the Maine woods — a real person, deeply involved in the affairs of his tribe and eventually ousted in a split that saw the Penobscots divided into two groups — the Old Party and the New Party — that the Maine Legislature forced to alternate turns in power in order to establish peace. Yet controversial as he was, John Neptune remains larger than life in the perceptive and poetic portrait that Mrs. Eckstrom draws of him.

No description of Maine people would be complete without a bow to Yankee ingenuity — or inventiveness might be a better term. The Stanley brothers of Kingfield stand out in that category. They were born in the northern Franklin County town on June 1, 1849 — identical twins named Francis E. and Freeland O. — and they have left their surname to posterity in the immortal "Stanley Steamer" the pioneer automobile that they developed and perfected.

That the automobile industry turned in a direction away from steam has proved to be unfortunate in these days of international oil crises, but no doubt it was inevitable when the Stanley brothers were alive. In the early years of automobile manufacture, they set speed and endurance records, only to see their crafted vehicles fail to keep up with the competition of mass production as introduced by Henry Ford. Their contribution however, to the development of the automobile in America was considerable and is remembered to this day.

Finally, there is the notable Mainer who is never notable at all, except in a local sense. Every community in Maine has personalities whom it remembers and about whom stories are frequently told, if they are not themselves always telling entertaining stories that are long remembered.

Like "Uncle" Curt Morse, the lobsterman and local humorist in Washington County. One of his favorite stories, like so many Maine stories, concerns the gullibility of those from "away", the city slickers who come to Maine and really don't know very much. In this case, it had to do with an anchor that Curt found caught up in his lobster gear, a heavily corroded anchor that looked much bigger and heavier than it was due to the incrustations of sea life and rust on it. In fact, some New Yorkers in the area were absolutely amazed to see Curt hoist it up onto his shoulder and carry it off, after they had just bet with each other that it would weigh at least ten tons. When they expressed their astonishment to Curt, he told them. "Oh, the heft o' it don't amount to much. Fact is, when I see a heavy storm comin' up, I always take my boat under my other arm."

The New Yorkers went off, arguing about the anchor, and one of them said he would have the story put in a New York paper with the headline, "Man Lugs Ten Ton Anchor Up Across a Field". The other New Yorker said it was a good thing the ground in that field was hard and dry; otherwise, Curt would have gone right into the ground with that much weight on his back.

Serious and humorous, heroic and talented, the diverse persons in these thumbnail sketches are but a sampling of Maine people, hundreds of whom could be written about here. English or French, Indian or Irish, whatever their origin, they all now operate within the "Yankee" mold, (remembering that Yankee comes from *Yenghi*, an Abnaki Indian word). Maine without its unique and still evolving population of Maine people would simply be a stretch of beautiful land covered with lots of trees. Its spirit has to be that of those — illustrious as well as unnoted — who have lived here and contributed in the past, or who live here now and keep up the sense of Maine that these forebearers have created.

Additional Essay Questions

THE ALLAGASH

Henry David Thoreau may have been the first naturalist to bring the Allagash to public notice when he praised its beauty in his book, *The Maine Woods*.

Today, the Allagash, although small for a Maine river, is one of the most celebrated water courses in the State and perhaps the best known Maine river out-of-state. During the 1950's and 1960's, when its pristine quality was threatened by several dam proposals, conservationists throughout the nation rallied to the cry of "Save the Allagash." The State, unwilling to have the Federal government step in, finally took action itself, and created the Allagash Wilderness Waterway, a corridor of publicly-controlled land where within 250 feet on each side of the river, the Bureau of Parks and Recreation maintains a protective zone and has some jurisdiction within a mile on either side.

The Allagash is a major sub-drainage of the far bigger St. John River. It is about 62 miles in length from Eagle Lake to the river's confluence with the St. John. Two dams suggested on the St. John at Cross Rocks and Rankin Rapids would have flooded the Allagash. These projects were eventually abandoned to be replaced by another proposal farther downstream on the St. John at Dickey and Lincoln School. This controversial hydroelectric scheme, which would not have flooded the Allagash, has been deauthorized by Congress, except for the much smaller dam planned for Lincoln School. However, opposition still continues against the Lincoln School dam.

The Allagash is famed for its wilderness canoe trips. It is also noted for its native brook trout, populating the river as well as the numerous ponds and lakes connected with the system. Lake trout ("togue" to Maine people) are found in the deep waters of the larger lakes. Allagash Falls helps prevent yellow perch and other warm water fish from ascending to the Upper Allagash where they would provide serious competition to the native trout.

With the creation of the waterway, canoe traffic has increased on the Allagash. Some people complain that its wilderness quality has suffered. Be that as it may (and such judgments are always subjective), the action of Maine government in affording the protection it has given to this waterway has been a milestone in conservation history. It has been followed by other similar ground-breaking actions, like the creation of the Saco River Corridor on another important canoeing river in Maine and the comprehensive "Rivers Legislation" passed in 1983 by the 111th Legislature, which guarantees protection to almost all of Maine's major rivers and many of its lesser ones.

1. *Who wrote* The Maine Woods?

2. *About how long is the Allagash?*

3. *What agency of Maine government administers the Allagash Wilderness Waterway?*

4. *Name one of the dams, which if built, would have flooded the Allagash.*

5. *What governmental mechanism protects the Saco River?*

A brook trout, the most common game fish in the Allagash watershed.

1. **Henry David Thoreau.**

2. **62 miles.**

3. **The Bureau of Parks and Recreation.**

4. **Cross Rocks, Rankin Rapids.**

5. **The Saco River Corridor.**

Canoists on the Allagash River.

Additional Essay Questions

NEAL DOW

In 1815, when Neal Dow was eleven years old, the first total abstinence society in the world was founded in his hometown of Portland, Maine. In 1834, its partisans launched the first state prohibition movement. Already, by then, young Neal Dow had made his mark as a temperance campaigner when he publicly protested the serving of liquor at an anniversary celebration of the Portland Volunteer Fire Department. At this time, in 1827, he had been a member of the department for five years and he was to become its chief engineer during the 40 years that he remained one of its volunteers.

In 1846, Dow was instrumental in having the nation's first prohibition statute pushed through the Maine Legislature. Two years later, he was chosen to be President of the National Temperance Society. He was elected Mayor of Portland in 1851 and stayed in that post until 1859. It was in 1851 that he successfully lobbied for an even tougher prohibition law in Maine than the one passed in 1846. This highly restrictive measure became known nationally as "The Maine Law."

Dow was subject to a great deal of abuse, both verbal and physical. He was, however, greatly skilled at boxing and always in fine physical condition. As Mayor, he was attacked one day by a drunken rowdy whom he laid flat with a single punch to the chin. On another occasion, he personally disarmed a drink-crazed man who was holding four policemen at bay with a pistol.

Although a Quaker, Dow volunteered to fight in the Civil War. He was made Colonel of the 13th Maine Regiment and soon advanced to Brigadier-General. At the Battle of Port Hudson in Louisiana, he was wounded twice by Confederate sharpshooters, then captured and kept at Richmond's Libby Prison until exchanged in 1864 for General Fitzhugh Lee, a nephew of Robert E. Lee.

In later life, Dow was a candidate for President of the United States on the Prohibition Party ticket in 1880. He travelled worldwide to lecture on temperance issues and served as President of the World Temperance Union. He died on October 7, 1897 at the age of 93.

1. *What position did Neal Dow eventually hold in the Portland Volunteer Fire Department?*

2. *When did Neal Dow become President of the National Temperance Society?*

3. *How long was Neal Dow mayor of Portland?*

4. *What was the military outfit that Neal Dow commanded during the Civil War?*

5. *In what Southern city was Neal Dow kept as a prisoner of war?*

Neal Dow's home in Portland on upper Congress Street, today a museum.

Neal Dow, the father of prohibition and mayor of Portland, 1851–59.

1. **Chief engineer.**

2. **1848.**

3. **Eight years (1851–1859).**

4. **The 13th Maine Regiment.**

5. **Richmond, Virginia.**

Additional Essay Questions

THE FIRST NAVAL BATTLE OF THE AMERICAN REVOLUTION

Machias, which is an Indian name meaning "Bad Little Falls," was settled early in the history of Maine — as early as 1633. But the trading station the English erected there then was destroyed by the French. Subsequently, the pirate Samuel Bellamy tried to use the location for his abortive "Pirate Republic." Not until 1763, after the French left Canada, was a successful English settlement established.

The tough fishing and trading folk who came to live in this exposed outpost were staunch partisans of American independence. When, in June 1775, an arrogant British naval captain named Moore ordered them to take down a Liberty Pole they'd erected, they reacted as might be expected. They decided to seize Moore and his armed sloop, the "Margaretta." However, the British officer — described as "a slip of a boy" — somehow learned that the patriots were coming to capture him while he was at church on Sunday morning, June 11 and he slipped out a window and rowed back to his ship. Soon, he opened fire on the town with his cannon, but did no damage.

The Americans met at O'Brien's Brook and debated what to do. Their arguments were long-winded and inconclusive until, with a dramatic gesture, Colonel Benjamin Foster changed the mood. He stepped across the brook and challenged those in favor of action to follow him. All did. The stream to this day is known as "Foster's Rubicon."

The next day, armed with pitchforks, axes and fowling pieces, 40 local men piled into the sloop, "Unity," commanded by Jeremiah O'Brien, and attacked the "Margaretta." The haughty Captain Moore was shot and the British, getting the worst of the hand-to-hand combat, soon surrendered. The wounded enemy were brought ashore to Burnham's Tavern, where Captain Moore expired. He was later buried in the O'Brien cemetery. The "Margaretta," rechristened the "Machias Liberty" went out to sea again as an American warship, tracking down two more British vessels and capturing them both. Finally, these Machias searovers turned all three of their prizes over to the Continental Navy.

Burnham's Tavern still stands today as does the O'Brien homestead, which is currently the residence of the president of the University of Maine at Machias. Jeremiah O'Brien's father Morris had fought with Maine's own William Pepperrell at the seige of Louisburg in 1745.

---

1. *What does Machias mean in the Indian language?*

2. *What did Captain Moore order the Americans to do?*

3. *What was the original name of Foster's Rubicon?*

4. *How many men went to attack the British?*

5. *On what date was the "Margaretta" attacked and captured?*

Burnham's Tavern in Machias. It was here that the captain of the British sloop "Margaretta' expired of his wounds after the first naval battle of the Revolution.

1. "Bad Little Falls".

2. Take down their Liberty Pole.

3. O'Brien's Brook.

4. 40 men.

5. June 12, 1775.

The earthworks at Fort O'Brien, built on the site of Fort Machias, and named for one of the heroes of the "Margaretta" battle.

Additional Essay Questions

THE STATE CAPITAL

When Maine became a state in 1820, the state capital was in Portland, where in several buildings the Legislature and the 190 persons who comprised the Executive and the Judiciary were housed. Yet it had never been intended by those who formed Maine that Portland should remain the capital. So in 1821, a joint legislative committee was chosen to select a new site.

Their first choice was Hallowell. But political considerations soon torpedoed Hallowell, which was then the largest community on the Kennebec. Hallowell's political problem was that it was a hotbed of Federalist Party strength while the Legislature was controlled by the opposition Democrat-Republicans (we would call them plain Democrats today). Thus, a new search committee was initiated.

The next choice was Weston's Hill in Augusta, a strategic elevation overlooking the river on the road from Hallowell. They further recommended that the Legislature meet there within five years, which would have meant 1827. Portland legislators delayed this timetable. In 1825, the Legislature was still debating the issue. Even the eloquence of Augusta's Reuel Williams, later to be a U.S. senator, could not stave off a 65-64 defeat of the Augusta plan in the House. But in 1827, Augusta finally had the votes and Portland outsmarted itself through some political maneuvering that didn't work out. A building commissioner was chosen (he was William King, the state's first governor) and $60,000 was raised by selling off 10 townships in the wildlands. Charles Bulfinch, one of America's foremost architects was hired and on the Fourth of July, 1829, the cornerstone of the capitol was laid.

In 1832, the building was completed, but a cost overrun of $30,000 allowed Portland to open up the question again of moving the capital. They did so also in 1837, 1860, in 1889 and even as late as 1907. The strongest effort by Portland was the last one, which had been sparked by Governor William Cobb's request for a new state office building. The senate approved a committee recommendation to remove the capital to Portland. This was followed by a battle royal in the House. By only eight votes, the House defeated the attempt.

Several years later, Augusta lawmakers saw to it that an amendment to the state constitution was prepared, stating that Augusta would be the capital of Maine. The voters approved. Bulfinch's handsome granite State House and the rest of the seat of government obviously will remain in place.

---

1. *In 1821, what city was the first choice for the new capital?*

2. *What site in Augusta was chosen for the capitol?*

3. *How many votes defeated Augusta's efforts in 1825?*

4. *Who designed the capitol building?*

5. *When was the last attempt to move the capital to Portland?*

The chamber of the Maine House of Representatives inside the State House.

Aerial view of Maine's capitol complex in Augusta.

1. **Hallowell.**

2. **Weston's Hill.**

3. **One vote.**

4. **Charles Bulfinch.**

5. **1907.**

Additional Essay Questions

FARMING IN MAINE

The year 1880 was the high point for farming in Maine. The number of farms had reached almost 65,000 and 6.6 million acres was in production. The average farm in those days was about 100 acres. The total value of farming in Maine was then about $22 million.

Contrast these figures with the present. Only about 7,600 farms are at work in Maine, farming only about 1.7 million acres. The average size of these farms is 225 acres. And the total value is more than $400 million.

Agriculture ranks third after pulp and paper and food processing in its contribution to the Maine economy. A wide variety of products is raised. Surprisingly, the most valuable is not the renowned Maine potato, but the egg, which in 1979 reached a value of over $100 million, almost a quarter of total farm value. Egg raising has seen a spectacular growth in Maine, their production increasing by 60 percent between 1967 and 1975. The world's largest "brown egg" operation is in Maine, which devotes 75 percent of its egg production to New England's traditional preference for brown eggs.

Potatoes are the next most valuable farm product. Maine is the number one producer in the country of certified seed potatoes and third in overall potato growing. About 90 percent of the more than $90 million worth of production is done in Aroostook County.

Dairying is also big business in Maine, with 1,265 commercial dairy farms. Milk production per cow has increased dramatically from 7,500 pounds in 1960 to 10,300 pounds in 1975. Augusta, Maine has the highest per capita milk consumption in the United States.

In recent years, Maine's important broiler industry has suffered a decline. Several broiler packing plants have gone out of business. The high cost of feed, which must be imported from out of state, is a crucial factor.

Other important crops in Maine are apples and wild blueberries. In fact, Maine is the number one producer of wild blueberries in the United States. The crop comes from 40,000–50,000 acres of low bush barrens, mostly in Washington County. Apple production is located primarily in southwestern Maine. The prime variety raised is the McIntosh, which accounts for about two-thirds of all apples sold.

Maine farmers also raise beef cattle, vegetables (for the increasing roadside market), some oats, hay, hogs, and a few sheep and lambs.

The largest number of farms are in Aroostook County, followed by Penobscot and Kennebec.

---

1. *About how many farms were there in Maine in 1880?*

2. *What is the average size of a Maine farm today?*

3. *What type of eggs do most Maine producers raise?*

4. *Are blueberries in Maine mostly high bush or low bush?*

5. *Which Maine county has the second highest number of farms?*

Blueberries. Maine is the nation's largest commercial producer.

Dairy cows at a farm in China, Maine.

Potato Queen aboard a tractor.

1. **65,000.**

2. **225 acres.**

3. **Brown eggs.**

4. **Low bush.**

5. **Penobscot County.**

Additional Essay Questions

3

TWO MODERN LEADERS

Margaret Chase Smith

The doughty lady from Skowhegan has added to Maine's impressive list of "firsts." She was the first woman to serve in both the U.S. House and Senate, the first Republican woman elected to the upper chamber, the first woman senator not merely appointed to fill out a term and the first woman whose name was put in nomination for president by a major political party.

Margaret Chase Smith entered politics when she married Clyde H. Smith, state legislator and publisher, whose secretary she had been. When Smith was elected to Congress, the couple moved to Washington, D.C. and four years later, after his death, she was named to succeed him. She served four terms in the House and went to the Senate after a difficult Republican primary in which she defeated two ex-governors.

In the Senate, Mrs. Smith became known for several things. She was famous for wearing a fresh red rose every day; more substantially, she built a reputation for almost never missing a roll call vote. Her most celebrated moment came in 1950 with her "Declaration of Conscience" speech, aimed at the tactics of Senator Joseph McCarthy of Wisconsin.

In 1983, the Democrat-controlled 111th Legislature honored Mrs. Smith with a "Margaret Chase Smith Day." A library containing her papers and memorabilia is open to the public is Skowhegan.

Edmund S. Muskie

The son of Polish immigrants, a Democrat in Maine in an era of Republican domination, Ed Muskie came as close to being President of the United States as any Mainer since James G. Blaine.

In 1954, he was the surprise victor for governor on the Democratic ticket. He then went on to capture the U.S. Senate seat and stayed in that body for 22 years, carving a solid record of accomplishment in the environmental field, foreign relations and budget matters.

It was no surprise to Maine people when in 1968, Hubert Humphrey chose him to be his vice presidential running mate. Some experts feel that if the ticket had been reversed that year, the Democrats would have won. Four years later, Muskie was not able to capture the presidential nomination due in part to what were later revealed as "dirty tricks" perpetrated by the Nixon Administration.

In 1980, Ed Muskie resigned from the Senate and became President Jimmy Carter's secretary of state.

---

1. *Where is Margaret Chase Smith from in Maine?*

2. *When did she object to Senator McCarthy's "red-baiting" tactics?*

3. *In what year was Ed Muskie first elected governor of Maine?*

4. *Who appointed him to be secretary of state?*

5. *What flower did Margaret Chase Smith always wear?*

---

1. **Skowhegan.**

2. **1950.**

3. **1954.**

4. **President Jimmy Carter.**

5. **A red rose.**

Portrait of Margaret Chase Smith, U.S. Senator 1949–73, the first woman ever to have her name placed in nomination for President by a major political party.

Additional Essay Questions

THE FISHING INDUSTRY

Lobsters were once so plentiful in Maine that they could be picked up live on the beaches. In the 18th century, a contract with a servant had to include a clause that lobster would not be used more than three times a week for the servant's food. Even in the middle of the 19th century, lobsters were still being used for fish bait by Maine fishermen.

Today, lobsters are by far the most valuable species in the entire Maine catch. Using 1979 figures, the value of the lobster catch was close to $40 million. All *fish* landed did not even add up to $25 million. Yet lobsters have their ups and downs. In 1977, a dismal season for them, their total value was less than seven million dollars.

Overall, Maine's fishing industry during the 1970's showed a steady, even spectacular growth, more than doubling from 1970 to 1979, going from $30.6 million to $80.2 million.

Among the different species of fish caught, the flounder appeared to be the most valuable. However, there are 13 different types of flounder that are counted in the catch, including blackbacks, sea dabs, flukes, gray sole, lemon sole, sand flounder and yellowtails, and large, small and medium varieties of each. In terms of poundage, the sea herring — the vaunted Maine sardine — leads the pack with almost 90 million pounds in 1979. The sardine has been a frustrating industry for Maine, once so plentiful that there were many canning factories Down East, then disappearing, then reappearing.

The same is true for Maine shrimp. In the 1960's, it was felt that the decrease of temperature in Maine waters would make this arctic creature a major fishery in the Gulf of Maine. In

A typical lobster boat, showing the "steadying sail" used in certain Maine waters.

1978, it had so disappeared that only 125 pounds were caught for a total value of $12. Then, the following year, the shrimp began coming back; or at least more than 72,000 pounds were caught.

Soft-shelled clams — "steamers" — are the next most single valuable Maine salt water product after lobsters. Between five million and six million pounds are annually harvested.

Commercial fishing in Maine covers a wide range of species and being added to it are products produced by aquaculture, particularly mussels, which continue to gain in use. The Department of Marine Resources, in addition to enforcing marine laws, actively encourages aquaculture and the utilization of species that previously were ignored or wasted.

---

1. *How many times a week could you feed your servant lobster in Maine in the 18th century?*

2. *What was a bad year for lobsters in Maine?*

3. *Name two types of flounders.*

4. *In 1978, only 125 pounds of Maine shrimp were caught. How much were they worth?*

5. *What agency of Maine government regulates the fishing industry?*

Lobster traps, piled to dry.

1. **Three.**

2. **1978.**

3. **The types are: blackbacks, sea dabs, flukes, gray sole, lemon sole, sand flounder and yellowtail.**

4. **$12.**

5. **Department of Marine Resources.**

Additional Essay Questions

BAILEY'S MISTAKE

Some maps don't mark it, but the staid and proper Coast and Geodetic Survey of the U.S. Department of Commerce has put down this little seacoast village in Washington County by its local nickname of Bailey's Mistake. A favorite comparison of different sand colors in the county's beaches uses the term, as has already been done here for a Toss-Up Question: red at Perry, white at Jonesport and black at Bailey's Mistake.

The area is located seven miles west of Lubec. It was settled in the early 1800's and incorporated in 1827 as "Trescott." As in most of these Down East towns, the inhabitants fished, farmed, logged and built an occasional ship.

Then, one stormy night in 1830, an incident took place that was to give Trescott its change of name. An experienced skipper from Boston named Bailey was heading for Lubec in a four-masted schooner. Confident of the use he had made of his sextant and compass, despite the thick, swirling fog, he steered toward some narrows that he thought had to be the Lubec Peninsula and Campobello Island. Shortly, afterward, his vessel ground to a shuddering halt, having run onto a ledge that to this day is known as Bailey's Ledge.

When the fog cleared the next morning, Bailey and his crew could see no sign of Lubec. Instead, they found themselves stranded in the center of a mile-wide bay at the end of which was a tiny settlement of houses with fish weirs, a few ship-building docks and a lumber mill — Trescott, in other words, which, although the captain didn't know it then, had been silently converted into "Bailey's Mistake."

Bailey never went back to Boston. Too embarrassed to face his home office, he unloaded his cargo of lumber and then as soon as he had floated free, used the boards to build homes for himself and some of his crew and stayed in Bailey's Mistake for the rest of his days.

1. *How many miles from Lubec is Bailey's Mistake?*

2. *In what U.S. Department is the Coast and Geodetic Survey?*

3. *Where was Bailey coming from?*

4. *When did the famous incident of Bailey's Mistake take place?*

5. *Where did Bailey go aground?*

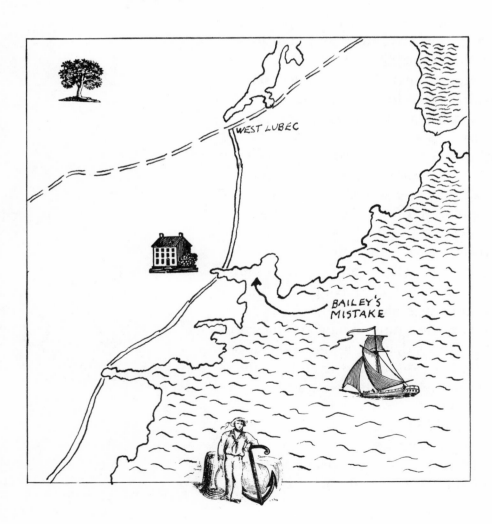

1. **Seven miles.**

2. **Department of Commerce.**

3. **Boston.**

4. **1830.**

5. **On Bailey's Ledge.**

A QUICKY

Two out-of-state duck hunters were trying out a new bird dog in Maine. When they shot their first duck, they were amazed to see this new dog walk right out on top of the water to retrieve the prey and come back in the same manner across the surface. They could hardly believe their eyes. The same thing happened with the next bird they shot. But who would believe that their dog could walk on water? They needed some impartial witnesses.

Then along came two Maine hunters. The out-of-staters cordially offered them the use of their dog. The Mainers shot several ducks. Each time the dog walked on water to get them and bring them back. However, the Mainers made not a single comment.

Unable to contain himself any longer, one of the out-of-staters blurted to them, "What's the matter with you two? Don't you notice anything unusual about our dog?"

"Sure do," said one of the Mainers. "Didn't know if we should tell you or not. That foolish animal can't swim."

Additional Essay Questions

THOMAS BRACKETT REED

He was 6 feet 3 inches tall and weighed almost 300 pounds, a giant of a man — "Czar Reed," as he was called in the days when he presided over the United States House of Representatives as the most powerful speaker it has ever had.

Portland-born, Bowdoin-educated Tom Reed was actually first admitted to the bar as a lawyer in San Jose, California. But he did not stay out West for long. After a short stint on an ironclad Union warship patrolling the Mississippi during the Civil War, he came back to Portland in 1865 to hang out his barrister's shingle.

Soon, he went into politics. Two terms were spent in the State House of Representatives, then a term as Attorney General and he presently moved on to Washington. He arrived in 1876 and stayed for the next 23 years.

"Reed's Rules," which he perfected during his reign as speaker, are the parliamentary guidelines that the Maine Legislature uses today. One of Reed's most noteworthy impositions of the tremendous authority he had came when he broke the habit of the opposition of blocking all House business by refusing to answer quorum calls. Reed shattered tradition one day by simply declaring that the silent members were "present."

Everyone feared his wit, which was as sharp as his friend Mark Twain's. "A statesman," he once declared, "is a successful politician who is dead." He lectured a representative from Massachusetts by saying to him, "Russell, you do not understand the theory of a five minute debate. The object is to convey to the House either information or misinformation. You have consumed several periods of five minutes without doing either." When a congressman jumped up and cried, "I was thinking, Mr. Speaker, I was thinking." Reed shot back, "No one will interrupt the gentleman's commendable innovation." After he had left one victim speechless, he declared, "Having embedded that fly in the liquid amber of my remarks, I will proceed."

In 1896, Reed unexpectedly lost the Republican presidential nomination to William McKinley. A devoted anti-imperialist, he was shocked enough by the outbreak of the Spanish-American War to resign his seat in disgust. His last three years were spent shuttling between his home in Portland and his law office in New York City.

Thomas Brackett Reed of Portland, speaker of the U.S. House of Representatives in the late 1800's, the redoubtable "Boss Reed," whose "Reed's Rules" serve as the parliamentary procedure for the present-day Maine Legislature and many other legislative bodies.

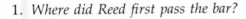

1. *Where did Reed first pass the bar?*

2. *How tall was he?*

3. *How many years was he in Congress?*

4. *He was supposedly as witty as what famous writer?*

5. *To whom did he lose the Republican presidential nomination?*

1. **San Jose, California.**

2. **6 feet 3 inches.**

3. **23 years.**

4. **Mark Twain.**

5. **William McKinley.**

MAKE UP YOUR OWN QUESTIONS

Throughout the book, sections like "What You Ought To Know About Maine," the "Quickies," even the material in the answers and questions, themselves (particularly the "Essay Questions") offer opportunities for you, the reader, to devise your own questions.

In addition, the following section contains facts about Maine, arranged in no particular order, that can also serve as raw material for formulating questions should the need or desire arise.

Selected Maine tide heights

(average rise in feet)

Calais	20
St. Croix Is.	19.6
Eastport	18.2
W. Quoddy Head	15.7
Bangor	13.1
Jonesport	11.5
Bucksport	11
Bar Harbor	10.5
Sedgwick	10.2
Castine	9.7
Owl's Head	9.4
Portland	9
Kittery Point	8.7
Bath	6.4
Gardiner	5
Brunswick	3.8

Maine's largest islands

Mount Desert	68,973 acres
Deer Isle	17,750 acres
Vinalhaven	12,823 acres
Georgetown	11,069 acres
Islesboro	7,192 acres
Swans	6,883 acres
North Haven	6,713 acres
Isle au Haut	6,576 acres

Some old bridges

Babb's Bridge	South Windham, built 1864, burnt 1973, restored; the oldest covered bridge in Maine.
Sunday River Bridge	Newry, built 1872.
Lovejoy Bridge	South Andover, built 1868.
Bennett Bridge	Lincoln Plantation, built 1901.
Low's Bridge	Sangerville, built 1857.
Robyville Bridge	Corinth, built 1876.
Watson Settlement Bridge	Littleton, built 1911.
Sewall's Bridge	York, built 1761; the oldest pile bridge in America.

Some key dates

1003	Leif Erikson explores the Maine coast.
1497	Voyages of the Cabots undertaken. Establish English claims to Maine.
1524	Verrazano establishes claim for France.
1604	St. Croix Island settlement by French.
1605	Waymouth kidnaps five Main Indians.
1607	Popham Beach settlement by English.
1609	Jesuit mission set up by French on Penobscot Bay.
1614	Captain John Smith maps the New England coast.
1632	England cedes Acadia to France.
1639	Maine is granted to Sir Ferdinando Gorges.
1652	Massachusetts takes over Maine.
1675	King Philip's War.
1677	Massachusetts buys the claims of Gorges' heirs.
1691	New Massachusetts Charter given by William and Mary designates Maine a "District."
1692	Serious Indian raids on Maine. York "massacre."
1704	Colonel Church attacks Indians in north.
1718	Bellamy's brief pirate "Republic" at Machias.
1724	Colonials raid on Norridgewock kills the Jesuit Father Rasle and decimates Indians.
1725	Battle of Lovewell's Pond.
1741	New Hampshire becomes a separate Province; border with Maine established.
1745	Louisbourg captured by colonial troops commanded by William Pepperrell of Kittery.
1748	English hand back Louisbourg to French in Treaty of Aix-la-Chapelle.
1763	Treaty of Paris. France surrenders all claims to North America.
1775	First naval battle of Revolution at Machias.
1775	Benedict Arnold's march to Quebec.
1777	The "Ranger" built at Kittery.
1779	Defeat of the Penobscot Expedition.
1783	Treaty of Versailles fixes Maine's boundary.
1812	British attack Maine, occupy Down East coast.
1820	Maine separates from Massachusetts, becomes a state.
1832	Augusta becomes state capital.
1838	"Aroostook War" commences.
1842	Webster-Ashburton Treaty settles boundary question.
1851	"The Maine Law." First strong prohibition statute in U.S.
1860–65	Civil War. 73,000 Maine men serve.
1868	First wood pulp produced in Maine, starting paper industry here.
1866	Great Portland fire.
1884	James G. Blaine runs for president.
1898	Battleship Maine blown up.
1900	Maine population reaches almost 700,000.
1910	Final boundary dispute with Canada settled.
1919	Acadia National Park created.
1936	Only Maine and Vermont vote against Roosevelt.

1951	First state sales tax.
1956	Maine Turnpike opened from Kittery to Portland.
1960	Election changed from September to November.
1968	Super University of Maine created.
1971	State government reorganized.
1979	Norse coin found.
1980	Indian land claims settled.

Maine's tallest mountains

Katahdin, Baxter Peak	5,267 feet
Katahdin, Hamlin Peak	4,751 feet
Sugarloaf	4,237 feet
Old Speck	4,180 feet
Crocker	4,168 feet
Bigelow, West Peak	4,150 feet
North Brother	4,143 feet
Saddleback	4,116 feet
Bigelow, Avery Peak	4,088 feet
Abram	4,049 feet
The Horn (Saddleback)	4,023 feet
Crocker, South Peak	4,000 feet

Some Maine "Firsts"

First "Thanksgiving", 1607
First monastery and mission in New England, 1612.
First ship built in America, 1608.
First white flour mill in New England at Norway.
First woolen mill in New England at Brunswick.
First paper mill in New England near Bangor.
First pile bridge in America at York, 1761.
First gold found in America at Byron.
First American-born Royal Governor, Sir William Phipps.
First incorporated city in North America, Gorgeana (York).
First summer theatre in America, 1901.
First international telephone call, from Calais to St. Stephens, New Brunswick, 1881.
First transatlantic TV broadcast, from Andover, 1962.
First government fish hatchery, Bucksport, 1872.
First black bishop in America.
First sardine cannery, Eastport, 1876.
First environmental site selection law.
First oil conveyance protection law.
First alcohol premium law.
First woman elected to U.S. House and Senate.
First woman elected to Academie Francaise.

ILLUSTRATION CREDITS

The author and publisher gratefully acknowledge the following for use of illustrations:

Bangor Daily News: page 39.
Bates College News Bureau: page 33 top left.
State Representative Susan Bell: page 40 top.
Bowdoin College Museum of Art: page 166.

Central Photo Lab, State of Maine: pages 36 bottom; 89 center; 145 top; 189
Colby College: page 33 top right.
Colby College Art Museum: page 165.

William A. Farnsworth Library & Art Museum: page 164.

Robert H. Gardiner: page 146 bottom.

Henry A. Harding of York: pages 35 bottom center; 89 top; 95 bottom.
Mrs. Barbara Holt: page 144

Robert L. Johnston: pages 87 center; 105 top.

L. L. Bean: pages 105 bottom; 106.

Maine Department of Conservation: pages 112; 113; 180; 192 top.
Maine Department of Inland Fisheries & Wildlife: pages 57; 92; 93 left & right; 102 top & bottom; 103 top & bottom; 153 bottom; 179.
Maine Department of Marine Resources: page 43 top; 197, 198.
Maine Historic Preservation Commission: pages 33 top center & bottom left, right & center; 34 bottom; 35 center & bottom left & right; 36 top; 38; 90 top; 94 bottom; 95 top left; 96 top left & right; 149 top; 163 top; 182; 186; 203
Maine Publicity Bureau: pages 35 top; 36 center; 40 top; 41 bottom; 42 bottom; 43 center & bottom; 51; 87 top & bottom; 94 top; 96 bottom; 145 bottom; 146; 152 top & bottom; 153 top; 172; 185, 191, 192 bottom.
Maine State Museum: pages 33 center; 34 top; 41 top; 42 top; 44; 150 top; 151 bottom; 183; 194.

Ed Pert: page 188

Portland Press Herald: pages 55; 88 left & right; 89 bottom; 90 bottom; 95 top right; 143 top; 149 bottom; 150 bottom; 151 top; 170.

United Press International: page 50.

WCBB Channel 10: pages 7; 61; 115.
Mrs. Laura Elizabeth Wiggins: page 143 center.

INDEX

Gundalow: 89–90
Gunsmiths: 83–84
"Gurry": 83–84
"Gurrybutts": 83–84
"Gut bucket": 139–40
"Guzzle hole": 139–40

H
Hall, Robert Browne: 161–62
Hallowell: 187–89
Hamblin, Sturtevant J.: 158
Hamlin: town, 67–68; Hannibal, 17–18,
    48, 54, 66, 68, 124
Hampden: 171
Hamsters, Syrian: 123–24
Hancock: city, 162; county, 11–12;
    John, 12; warehouse, 12
"Hardscrabble": 29–30
Hardwood Island: 126
Harmon, Captain Johnson: 88
Harpswell: 58
Harris Dam: 146
Hartley, Marsden: 158, 166
Havey Crystals: 80
Hawthorne, Nathaniel: 16, 33, 34, 58,
    155
Head Tide: 79–80, 143
Healy, James Augustine: 169–71
Hemlock: 25–26, 117–18
Heron, great blue: 91, 93, 100
"Hiawatha": 88
Hiccups: 119–20
Hinckley, Newt: 3
Hispanics: 168
History, 44–51
"History of the District of Maine": 97
Hodge-Podge Board: 1
Holmes, Ezekiel: 82
Holy Ghost and Us Society: 147
"Home of Famous Sea Captains": 117–
    18
Homer, Winslow: 158–59
Home Rule: 108
Honeybee: 131–32
Hooker, Richard: 157
"Horse Soldiers"; 173
Houlton: 141–42
House of Representatives: Maine, 85–
    86, 107; U.S. 202–03
"House of Seven Gables": 155
How to play: 5–6
Howard: Oliver Otis, 48, 77–78;
    University, 78
Howe: Julia Ward, 143–44; Samuel
    Gridley, 143
Howells, William Dean: 156
"Hudson River School": 158

Huguenots: 132
Humphrey, Hubert H.: 195
Hunting: 23–24, 101
Hydropower: 135–36

I
Ice: 25–26
Ice cream: 133–34
Indian Affairs Bureau: 134
Indian Affairs Commissioner: 20
Indian chief: 19–20
Indian Island: 137–38
Indian land claims: 9–10, 38–39, 49–50,
    53, 132
Indian pudding, baked: 125–26
Indians: 26, 37–38, 44–46, 49–50, 52–
    53, 70, 87–88, 134, 137–38, 141–42,
    168, 175–76
Industry: 48–50
Inland Fisheries and Wildlife
    Department: 14, 98, 100, 101, 129
Ipcar, Dahlov: 159
Irish: 48, 167
Iroquois Confederation: 120
"Island of the Eagles": 130
Islands: 204
Isle au Haut: 20
"Isle of Bacchus": 133
Isles of Shoals: 18, 55, 138, 156
Italians: 44, 48, 167

J
"Jacking a deer": 27–28
Jackson: Andrew, 47, 74; Laboratory,
    123–24
"Jackson mice": 124
Jacques, Lt. Richard: 88
"Jag": 139–40
Jefferson, Thomas: 47
Jensen, Andy: 2
Jesuits: 37
Jewell Island: 54–55
Jewett, Sarah Orne: 127–28, 151, 154,
    156
Jewish: 167
John Hancock Wharf: 90
Johns Hopkins University: 66
Johnson: Andrew, 18, 78, 123–24, 150;
    Hiram, 57–58; Lyndon B., 124, 150
Jonesport: 71, 199
Jordan, Eben: 25–26
Jordan Marsh Company: 25–26
Joseph, Chief: 78
Josselyn: Henry, 173; John, 97, 127–28,
    173
Judiciary: 107–08, 187
"Julia and the Illuminated Baron":
    155

K
"Keep Cool": 155
Kellogg, Elijah: 157
Kennebago Lake: 66
Kennebec: County, 21–22, 71–72, 191;
    Indians, 87–88, 130; Journal, 16;
    River, 22, 25–26, 45, 129–30, 137–38,
    145–46
Kennebunk: 17, 117–18, 156
Kennebunkport: 134, 137–38, 156
Kennedy, John F.: 161–62
Kent: Edward, 68; Rockwell, 159, 165
Kidd, Captain: 54–55
Kiff, Captain: 55
King: Stephen, 58, 157; William, 47,
    71–72, 187
Kingdom, Incorporated: 147
King Philip's War: 37, 38–39, 121–
    22
King's Broad Arrow: 141
King William's War: 17
Kipling, Rudyard: 128, 133–34
Kittery: 17–18, 121–22
Knife Edge: 69–70
Knox: County, 11–12, 26, 75, 121;
    Henry, 12, 41, 118, 121–22, 155
Kotzschmar: Herman, 160–61;
    Memorial Organ, 160
Kuhn, Walt: 159
Ku Klux Klan: 169

L
"Lady of Maine": 154
"Lady of Massachusetts": 154
Lafayette: George Washington, 118;
    Marquis de, 117–18, 133; National
    Park, 118
Lakes: 23–24
Land agent: 111
Land-locked salmon: 23–24, 131
Lane, Fitz Hugh: 158, 163
Langlais, Bernard: 162
Laurent, Robert: 159
Law: 27–28
Lazy Lester: 119
Leavitt, Bud: 3
Lebanese: 167
Leblanc, Rene: 175
Lee: Fitzhugh, 182; Robert E., 182
Leeds: 77–78
Legislature: 10, 107–08, 112, 134, 181,
    187–89, 193, 202–03
Lewiston: 48, 73–74
Lex: 52
Lighthouse: 35–36
Lights of Fortune Round: 1
Lily Bay State Park: 67–68